WORLD CLUB

INTERMEDIATE

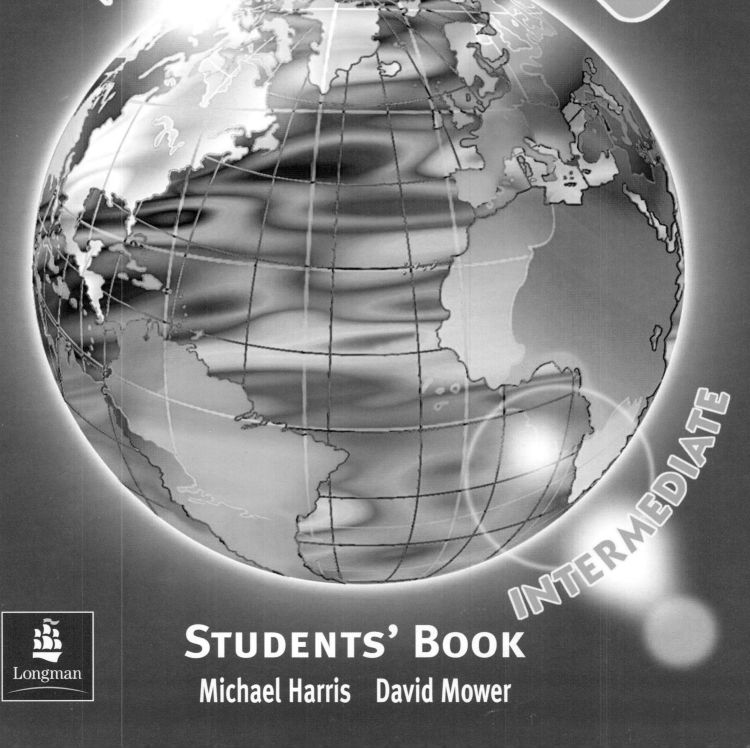

Longman

STUDENTS' BOOK

Michael Harris   David Mower

Summary of course content

Students' Book

Activity Book

A Your learning

a

Which of these topics are you interested in?

animals / fashion / cinema / houses / music / school / science / history / crime / families / holidays

Look at the module themes in this book (pages 2 and 3). Which of the topics you selected are included?

Example: fashion (module 1)

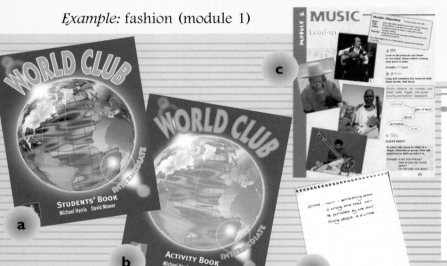

c

Which of these activities do you a) like doing?
b) think are very useful?

listening to the cassette
working in groups
speaking to a partner
reading
listening to stories
writing letters/stories
acting out situations
project
grammar games
pronunciation exercises
vocabulary exercises
Test Yourself activities

b

Look at the diagram and match the items with these descriptions.

Example: a = 2

1 The notebook where you put vocabulary and grammar notes.
2 The Students' Book.
3 A group of six lessons about one theme.
4 The book where you do practice activities.
5 A mini-dictionary in the Students' Book.
6 Where you assess your progress after each module.
7 The oral and written tasks at the end of each module.

d

Write five questions about the Students' Book.

Example: Who are in the photos in Lesson 2?

In pairs, ask and answer the questions.

B Vocabulary

a

WORD QUIZ

In pairs, choose the correct answers below:

1 Over a) 30% b) 60% c) 80% of the information in the world's computers is in English.
2 The most common word in English is a) *the* b) *hello* c) *sorry*.
3 The most common word for an English speaking five year-old is a) *you* b) *mummy* c) *I*.
4 The most common letter in English is a) s b) e c) r.
5 The words *cafeteria/cigar/potato/cannibal* all come from a) Italian b) French c) Spanish.

b

Look at the words taken from instructions in this book. Which are similar in your language?

nouns: description / mistake / activity / test / example / exercise / definition / questionnaire

verbs: decide / match / organise / use / discuss / ask / complete / answer / copy / guess / invent / compare

adjectives: important / true / false / correct / difficult / easy

c

Write down five instructions which are new for you in module 1.

Example: Read the article and match these headings with the paragraphs.

d

Organise your vocabulary book. Write down important words from this lesson and include:

• spelling
• part of speech (noun/verb, etc.)
• meaning (definition or translation)
• example sentence

Write the information, like this:

Crime: noun – something that is wrong and that can be punished by the law: Killing people is a crime.

e

In pairs, test your classroom vocabulary.

Example:

What does *guess* mean?
How do you spell *exercise*?
How do you *pronounce* this word?

C Grammar

'I only want to communicate in English Grammar is boring!'

NINA GHIZIKIS
ATHENS

a

Which of the people do you agree with?

CARLOS BLANCO
CÁCERES

PIA POSIO
GENEVA

'Grammar is very useful for learning a language, but it is not more important than communication.'

'I think grammar is the most important thing to learn. How can you communicate if you don't know the grammar?'

b

Match the grammar areas with the examples.

Example: 1 = c

1	question forms	a	*I get up at eight o'clock. / Now she's watching TV.*
2	negatives	b	*If the weather's good, we'll go.*
3	present tenses	c	*Which of them is it? / They're good, aren't they?*
4	past tenses	d	*It's made in Korea.*
5	future tenses	e	*I go <u>to</u> school <u>by</u> bus and get there <u>at</u> 8.30.*
6	perfect tense	f	*She's a good student, but her brother is better.*
7	prepositions	g	*I think Sue'll pass the exam but I'm going to fail!*
8	conditionals	h	*I've seen that film six times.*
9	passives	i	*I don't agree. I never arrive late.*
10	comparative	j	*When I came into the classroom, she was reading.*

c

Assess your use of each structure in exercise B.

A I understand and use it well.
B I sometimes make mistakes.
C I don't understand it.

d

In the grammar section of your notebook, write other examples of the structures from exercise B. Write translations in your own language.

D Listening and speaking

a

**Read this advice. Which things should you do:
a) before listening b) while listening?**

1 Get the general idea the first time you listen.
2 Read the questions and think about answers.
3 Use pictures to help you predict information about what you are going to hear.
4 Don't stop listening even if it is very difficult. Concentrate on what you *do* understand.

b

**Look at Linda and Mohammed. Guess
how old they are and what language(s) they are
studying. Then listen and check your guesses.**

c

**Copy the table, then listen again and
complete it.**

	Linda	Mohammed
Hours a week	*two*	
Years studied		
Problems		
Use outside class		

d

Match the problem with the advice.

1 You are speaking and you don't know a word
2 You can't think of what to say next

a Use expressions like: *well, you know . . .* and *really*.
b Think of another word that is similar or explain it in a few words e.g. *big car* instead of *lorry*.

e

**Make notes about these things. Then in
pairs, speak about yourself for as long
as possible.**

age / likes and dislikes / family /
hobbies / holidays / favourite music /
films / daily routine

Example: A: I'm seventeen. I really love the cinema, you know. Sometimes I go twice a week. I ...

E Reading and writing

a

Which of these things make reading easier?

a no pictures with the text
b an interesting topic
c knowing nothing about the subject
d having a dictionary for difficult words
e the words are very small
f not too many new words

b

Read the note. Copy and complete these networks with information about Alberto.

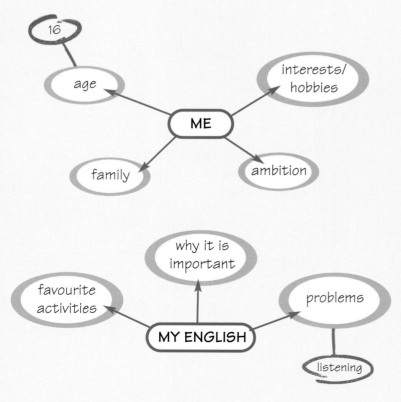

To: Ms Tomasini
From: Alberto Roca
Date: 23 September

AR

I'm sixteen and I have two sisters and one brother. We've got lots of animals at home, including a parrot called Tony who's fifty! I really like swimming so I go every day. Another thing I love is painting and drawing. When I leave school I don't want to go to university, I want to study to be a graphic designer.

I think English is important to get a job. If you are a designer, it is very useful to speak and understand some English. When we study English I like doing speaking activities, especially when we discuss things. The biggest problem for me is listening and often I don't understand the cassette.

c

Write a short note to your teacher, talking about yourself and your English.

Stage 1: Do a network like the one in exercise b to plan what you are going to write.

Stage 2: Use your plan to write a note to your teacher.

Stage 3: Check your note for mistakes and then give it to your partner to check.

Stage 4: Write a final version of the note.

FASHION

Lead-in

Module Objectives   In this module you will ...

Read a magazine article about top models, a poem and a fashion report

Talk about fashion and clothes, **practise** shopping and **describe** people

Listen to a dialogue, a documentary about fashion and cruelty to animals and a story

Revise using different tenses and auxiliary verbs

Your **final tasks** will be to **write** a fashion profile and to **interview** people about fashion.

b KEYWORDS

In groups, look at the list from an old magazine. Make a list of what is 'in' (fashion) now and what is 'out'.

In	Out
long hair	short hair
flared jeans	leather jackets
mini-skirts	long dresses
big earrings	rings
soul music	blues music
pink	dark colours

a  KEYWORDS

Which of these things can you see in the photographs? Use the mini-dictionary to help you.

> jeans skirt suit blouse trainers belt
> jacket shoes socks tie dress shirt
> sunglasses earrings T-shirt

Classify the clothes: smart / casual / either

Example: jeans = casual

c

Tell the class what your group thinks.

Example: We think that long hair is … **9**

1 Looking Good

A 🔑 KEYWORDS

Classify the words in the box: positive (+) or negative (-).

> smart nice horrible unfashionable awful
> attractive gross cool trendy tacky

B

In pairs, discuss what you think of the clothes in the photo on this page and on the *Lead-in* page.

Example: A: I think her jacket is smart.
B: So do I. And I like her skirt.
C: I don't. I think . . .

C 🗨

In pairs, ask and answer questions about buying clothes.

how often / when / where / who with

Example: A: How often do you buy clothes?
B: Not very often. I hate shopping!

D 📼

Look at the picture on the next page. Guess which of these things are true.

1 The boy doesn't like the jacket, because it is not dark enough.
2 He is looking for a jacket with big pockets.
3 He buys the jacket in the picture.
4 The girl is looking for a blue skirt.
5 She thinks the skirt is too long.
6 She buys the skirt in the picture.

Listen and check your guesses.

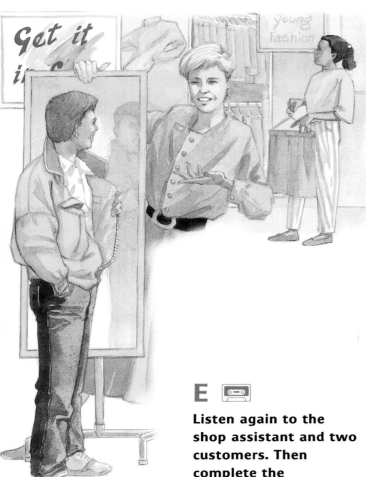

F

Look at this diagram. Prepare for a shopping situation, but do NOT write down the dialogue.

- (customer) Decide exactly what you are looking for.
  Example: dark blue jeans / size 42
- (shop assistant) Decide what clothes you have in your shop.
  Example: jeans / T-shirts / trainers
- Check vocabulary in the mini-dictionary.
- Practise saying expressions to yourself.
  Example: 'Can I help you?', 'I'm looking for ...'

E

Listen again to the shop assistant and two customers. Then complete the sentences below.

SHOP ASSISTANT	CUSTOMERS
From dialogue 1	
[1]... I help you?	No, thanks. I'm just [2]... How much is this?
It's [3]... pounds.	That's too [4]...
[5]... about this one?	I don't like the [6]... It's not [7]... enough.
That really suits you.	All right. I'll [8]... it.
From dialogue 2	
Can I [9]... you?	I'm [10]... for a skirt.
What [11]... are you?	I don't know. Can you measure me?
Would you like to try [12]... on?	Where are the changing [13]... ?
They're over there.	It's too [14]...

SHOP ASSISTANT	CUSTOMERS
Ask if you can help	Say what you're looking for
Ask about size	Give your size
Show clothes	Say why you don't like it/them
Suggest something else	Ask about price
Give the price	Ask to try it/them on
Say where the changing room is	Say you want to buy it/them

G

In pairs, take turns to practise buying something. Use the cues above to help you.

2 Top Models

A

Can you list the names of any well-known top models?

B

Read the article and match these headings with the paragraphs.

a International celebrities
b The need for glamour
c From schoolgirl to superstar
d In business

C

Read the article again and answer the questions about Claudia Schiffer.

1 Where did Michael Levaton discover her?
2 What film did she star in recently?
3 What is she going to do in the future?
4 What business does she run?
5 Why are she and other top models so famous?

Language Focus: Tense review

D

Match the tenses with the examples.

1	future with *going to*	a	Claudia now belongs to an exclusive club of supermodels ...
2	past simple	b	... now she is planning a career as an actress
3	present simple	c	Claudia Schiffer was an ordinary German schoolgirl ...
4	present continuous	d	They have also become successful businesswomen
5	present perfect	e	What is she going to do in the future?

Find more examples of these tenses in the magazine article.

Supermodel

1 Claudia Schiffer was an ordinary German schoolgirl from a small town near Düsseldorf when fashion agent Michael Levaton saw her dancing in a nightclub. A few months later Claudia was a fashion superstar. Now she is more famous than most Hollywood actresses.

2 Claudia belongs to an exclusive club of supermodels who have become international celebrities: Cindy Crawford, Naomi Campbell, Linda Evangelista, Kate Moss ... They jet around the world, they appear on TV chat shows and they have even started making films. Claudia Schiffer recently starred in the film *Blackout* and now she is planning a career as an actress. News of top models' private lives appears on the front pages of newspapers; like Naomi Campbell's turbulent romance with flamenco dancer Joaquín Cortés.

Celebrities

3 As well as being major celebrities, top models are not poor. Supermodels receive up to $30,000 for every appearance, and collect millions of dollars in advertising contracts. They have also become successful businesswomen. Claudia Schiffer, Elle MacPherson and Naomi Campbell run their own restaurant business together, the Fashion Café. 'It's our baby. We make all the decisions,' says Schiffer.

4 Why are these models so famous? After all, the only thing they do is try on clothes. Perhaps, in a world obssessed by image and style, they have the 'glamour' of the Hollywood stars of the 40s and 50s, which modern actresses just do not have. As Pauline Bernatchez of a Parisian modelling agency notes, 'Models seem more untouchable. People need glamour: they need to dream.'

E

Which tense do we use in these situations?

Example: 1 = present perfect

1 to talk about something in the past that is important now
2 to talk about the future
3 to describe what is happening now
4 to describe what people usually do
5 to talk about something that happened in the past

F

Put the verbs into the correct tense.

Example: 1 = has lived

Mark Stevens was born in 1973 in Connecticut and ¹... (live) there all his life. He ²... (be) an ordinary college student until 1992 when a photographer ³... (see) him in Washington Square Park in New York. He ⁴... (take) Mark's picture and it ⁵... (appear) in the prestigious 'Tell Magazine' a few months later. Since 1994 he ⁶... (work) for the Ford Modelling Agency. He ⁷... (have) a very busy schedule and at the moment he ⁸... (travel) a lot. Life as a model is not as easy as many people think. He ⁹... (work) very hard during the week and only ¹⁰... (relax) completely at the weekend. Mark has many plans for the future. First, he ¹¹... (plan) to finish his college course and then he ¹²... (look for) a job in the field of healthcare at the same time as modelling.

G

Imagine you are a famous model. In pairs, interview each other. Use these questions:

- Where are you from?
- How did you become a model?
- What have you done since then?
- What are you doing now?
- What is your lifestyle like?
- What are you planning to do in the future?

3 Appearance Matters

A

In pairs, discuss these questions.

1 How much does another person's appearance influence you?
   a not at all b a bit c a lot
2 Are you careful about your appearance?
   a never b sometimes c always
3 Do you ever:
   a dye your hair? b wear unconventional clothes? c have unconventional hair cuts?

B

Read the poem. How would Alfie answer question 3 in exercise A?

C

Read the poem again and answer these questions.

1 What is unusual about Alfie's appearance?
2 How do his teachers react to him?
3 What do other students think about his appearance?
4 What is Alfie's attitude?

ALFIE

My brother Alfie's had
his hair cut like a hedge,
it sticks up in the middle
and it's spiky round the edge.

5 He brushes it each morning
and keeps it fairly clean,
you'll see him when he's coming,
he's dyed it bottle green.

Now Alfie thinks he's trendy
10 he thinks he's really cool
looking like a football pitch
as he walks to school.

All the teachers hate him
because he's got green hair,
15 and other kids they laugh at him
but Alfie doesn't care.

by David Harmer

D

Imagine you have just met someone. Use the table below to write notes to describe him/her.

general appearance:	smart/tidy
physical appearance:	pretty/handsome/ unattractive
age:	young/middle-aged/old
hair:	blonde/dark/brown long/short
height:	tall/short/ medium height
build:	thin/slim/well-built/ overweight
complexion:	dark/fair

E

Read this dialogue. In pairs, act out a similar dialogue and find out about your partner's new friend.

A: I've just met this boy.

B: Oh, yes? What does he look like?

A: He's really handsome. He's tall and dark. He's got short hair. And he's got fantastic green eyes.

B: What kind of clothes does he wear?

A: He's very trendy. He wears jeans, trainers and leather jackets. He's cool and he's *very* nice!

B: Lucky you!

F

FAMOUS PERSON GAME

Each student thinks of a *very* famous person. In groups, ask questions and guess who it is.

Example: A: Is she pretty?
B: Yes, she is.
A: Is she dark?
B: No, she isn't.
A: Is she tall?
B: Yes, she is. Very tall.
A: Is she a supermodel?
B: Yes, she is.
A: Is it Claudia Schiffer?

4 Dressed to Kill

A

B

C

D

A

Look at the photos and match the animals with the products.

Example: 1 = B

B 🔑 KEYWORDS

Which of these things can you see in the photos?

> crocodile skin shoes   leather jacket   fur coat
> cotton trousers   ivory jewellery   woollen jersey
> cosmetics tested on animals   nylon shirt

C 📼

Are these things true or false?

1 There is a lot of cruelty to animals in the fashion industry.
2 We test shampoos on rats and monkeys.
3 You can buy 'cruelty-free' cosmetics and shampoos in some shops.
4 Dolphins are killed for their oil which is used in soaps.
5 No elephants are killed now because hunting is illegal.
6 Sometimes crocodiles are skinned alive and suffer a lot.

Listen to a radio interview and check your answers.

Language Focus: Auxiliaries

D

Listen again and complete the sentences with these words.

Example: 1 = is

do (x4) / have (x2) / is (x2) / don't (x2)

A: ¹... there cruelty to animals in the fashion industry?
B: Yes, there ²... .
A: They test things on animals, ³... they?
B: Yes, they ⁴... .
A: I think that's terrible.
B: So ⁵... I.
A: We kill lots of different animals for fashion products.
B: ⁶... we?
A: Literally thousands of elephants ⁷... died.
B: ⁸... they?
A: People ⁹... wear fur coats as much as before, ¹⁰... they?

E

Find examples of the following uses of auxiliaries in exercise D.

Example: a = 9

a   in negative sentences (e.g. I *don't* like it.)
b   in affirmative sentences (e.g. I*'ve* finished.)
c   in question tags (e.g. It*'s* terrible, isn't it?)
d   in short answers (e.g. Do you live here? Yes, I *do*.)
e   expressing surprise or interest (e.g. I love it. *Do* you?)
f   expressing agreement (e.g. I think it's fantastic. So *do* I.)
g   in questions (e.g. *Did* you buy that?)

F

In pairs, use the notes below to ask and answer questions.

Example: A: Do you think it's important to protect animals?
B: Yes, I do.
A: So do I.

1   think / important / to protect animals?
2   usually / buy / cruelty-free products?
3   ever / wear / animal products / like leather or fur?
4   ever / bought / ivory?
5   ever / seen / crocodile skin shoes?

G

In pairs, express opinions about the clothes you can see in photos and drawings in the first three modules of this book.

Example: A: That dress is great, isn't it?
B: No, I don't think so. But I think this jacket is nice.
A: Do you? I don't.

H 🅛 DICTIONARY SKILLS

Use the mini-dictionary to complete the table. If there is no information, the verb is regular.

VERB	PRESENT PARTICIPLE	PAST TENSE	PAST PARTICIPLE
dig	...	...	...
...	...	dyed	...
...	modelling	...	...
put on	...	...	...
...	...	...	slipped
...	winding up	...	...

5 Fluency

A

Listen to the story of Cinderella. When the story-teller pauses, correct the mistakes she has made.

Example: 1 Cinderella was poor. She didn't wear mini-skirts and leather jackets. She wore very old clothes.

Final Speaking Task: A Fashion Survey

B

Read these questions and add two more. In pairs, find out how fashion-conscious your partner is.

HOW FASHION-CONSCIOUS ARE YOU?

1 Do you ever read fashion magazines?
   a sometimes b often c never

2 Do you enjoy shopping for clothes?
   a Yes, a lot. b No, I hate it. c I quite like it.

3 Do you think designer labels are important?
   a yes b no

4 How important is it for you to wear fashionable clothes?
   **a very important b not at all important
   c only for special occasions**

5 Do you know what the fashionable colours are this year?
   a Yes, I do. b I think so. c No, I don't.

6 Would you wear a ring through your nose?
   a Yes, I would. b No, I wouldn't. c Maybe.

C

Look at the photos. What periods are they from?

FASH THROUGH

A After the First World War, the clothes of the twenties shocked many people. Fashions for women became more relaxed and freer than before. Women wore simple, comfortable clothes and the fashionable look was boyish. For example, young women had short hair and wore skirts above the ankle, which horrified many people. Clothes were colourful and informal, to match the new music and 'in' dances like the Charleston. Male fashion also became less formal. For instance, wealthy men began wearing suits. In the 1930s Hollywood stars became a major fashion influence and manufacturers began to mass-produce cheap, fashionable clothes.

ION
THE AGES

B In the eighteenth century, the French court at Versailles was the centre of the fashion world and clothes became very elaborate and exotic. For instance, women's dresses became wider. By the 1740s some fashionable dresses measured more than two metres across! Women also had enormous hairstyles with decorations like flowers and even fruit! In the 1770s in Britain, fashionable men copied the latest Italian styles. For example, they wore extravagant clothes, lots of pale make-up and wigs that were powdered and tied with ribbons.

D

Read the texts and answer these questions.

1 How did women's clothes change after the First World War?
2 What horrified people about women's clothes?
3 What was the 'in' dance in the 20s?
4 What influenced fashion in the 1930s?
5 Where was the centre of fashion in the eighteenth century?
6 What decorations did some women have on their hair?
7 What was unusual about fashionable men in the 1770s?

Find three ways of giving examples.

Example: dances *like* the Charleston

Final Writing Task: A Fashion Report

Fashion project

E

Write a fashion report for your school magazine.

Stage 1: Planning Choose a style in the past or present. Copy the table below and complete it with notes like these:

Characteristics	Examples
unusual hairstyles	spiky hair/dyed strange colours
unconventional clothes	big boots/torn jeans and T-shirts
music/lifestyles	aggressive punk rock

Stage 2: Writing Use your notes to write the description. Include ways of showing examples.

Stage 3: Checking When you have finished, give your description to your partner to check. Collect drawings or photos to illustrate it.

Grammar

A

Put the verbs in the correct tense.

Example: 1 = went

Inés Sastre is a top model and actress. She was born in Valladolid in 1973 and she ¹... (go) to a bilingual school, so she ²... (speak) French fluently as well as Italian and English.

She ³... (start) modelling when she was twelve. Then film director Carlos Saura ⁴... (choose) her for the film *El Dorado*.

In 1989 she ⁵... (win) the *Elle* supermodel contest but she ⁶... (not become) a full-time model because she wanted to continue her studies. After a degree in French literature, a film with Antonioni and some modelling in 1996 she ⁷... (become) the new face of *Trésor*, the famous Lancôme perfume.

Since then she ⁸... (be) very busy with modelling but she ⁹... (not accept) many films. However, at the moment she ¹⁰... (make) a film with Italian director Pupi Avati in which she ¹¹... (play) a character called Francesca Babini.

Now she ¹²... (live) in London, and she ¹³... (travel) a lot. In the next few months she ¹⁴... (make) another film. She ¹⁵... (also continue) her studies in medieval literature.

B

NOUGHTS AND CROSSES GAME

- **In pairs, copy the little grid.**
- **Choose a square in the box below then say a sentence using the tense indicated. If it is correct, put a nought or cross on the corresponding square in the little grid. Do not repeat any verbs. The first person to make a straight line is the winner.**

Example: Square 1 - future plan: "This weekend I'm going to do that history project."

future plan	future simple	present perfect
present simple	past simple	future plan
past simple	present perfect	present continuous

C

Complete this dialogue with auxiliaries.

Example: 1 = don't

A: I think that very short haircuts are terrible, ¹ ... you?
B: Yes, I ² ... . And I ³ ... never had a boyfriend with very short hair.
A: But I ⁴ ... like very long hair either.
B: Oh, I ⁵ ... , I love it. ⁶... you seen Tim recently?
A: No, I ⁷ ... .
B: He's got really long hair and he looks great.
A: ⁸ ... he? I never liked him much. He's quite shy, ⁹ ... he?
B: Yes, he ¹⁰ ... . But he's very interesting, when you talk to him!

Vocabulary

D 🔑 KEYWORDS

Complete a table for the words in the list.

NOUN	ADJECTIVE	OPPOSITE
fashion	fashionable	unfashionable

fashion / success / attraction / convention / tidiness / legality / formality

E KEYWORDS

**When would you wear these clothes?
Complete the table below.**

> leather jacket suit jeans T-shirt trainers
> smart shoes tie dress overcoat fur coat
> jersey belt skirt trousers denim jacket

Going out with friends	Going to a wedding	Never
leather jacket		

Pronunciation

F

Listen to these two vowel sounds.

Group 1	Group 2
/ ə / trousers	/ ɪ / jacket

**Copy the table and then listen and put the
words below into the correct group according
to the sounds.**

measure / painted / collar /leather / music /
shorter / pocket / colour / women / decorated /
freer / prettier / dresses / copied / enough /
aggressive / enormous / arrive

Listen again and repeat the words.

Test Yourself

A (8 points)

**Look at the notes about fashion model Nic
Eyre. Write sentences from the notes.**

Example: 1 Nic was born in 1975 and went to
school in Geneva.

1 born 1975 / go to school / Geneva
2 designer John Galiano discover him / 1993
3 1996 / make first film / *Long Evening*
4 now live / New York / work for an agency
5 travel a lot to Rome / Madrid / Paris
6 at the moment / make film in Sicily
7 make 3 films up to now / 2 with Russian director Ivan Tigorsky
8 next year plan / continue studies / law

B (7 points)

Complete these sentences with auxiliaries.

1 That jacket's really cool, ... it?
2 I ... not interested in fashion.
3 A: Monica's just won the competition.
   B: ... she? Wow!
4 A: Did you see that fashion show on TV?
   B: No, I ... .
5 A: I think that hairstyle is great.
   B: So ... I.
6 That's not very fashionable, ... it?
7 A: I've just passed the exam!
   B: ... you? That's great!

C (5 points)

Write the opposites of these words.

1 long
2 fashionable
3 successful
4 wealthy
5 conventional
6 tidy
7 formal
8 legal
9 nice
10 new

Extra Time

Look at Reading Club 1on page 96.

Module Check

Language Check

TENSE REVIEW

Present simple: Claudia Schiffer now **belongs** to an exclusive club of supermodels.

Present continuous: Claudia **is planning** a career as an actress.

Past simple: Michael Levaton **saw** Claudia dancing in a nightclub.

Present perfect: The supermodels **have** also **become** successful businesswomen.

Future (going to): She **is going to make** another film next year.

AUXILIARY REVIEW

Negatives: She **doesn't** like it.

Questions: **Did** she make that film?

Affirmative sentences: She **is** wearing a new dress.

Question tags: It's a fantastic dress, **isn't** it?

Short answers: Have you seen Jim? No, I **haven't**.

Surprise/interest: She's a model now. **Is** she?

Agreement: I think it's horrible. So **do** I.

Disagreement: I like that jacket. I **don't**.

Keyword Check

- **Make sure you know the meaning of these words and expressions.**
- **Put important new words in your vocabulary book.**

Clothes: skirt, dress, trousers, blouse, jeans, T-shirt, shirt, shoes, socks, trainers, belt, jacket, suit, tie, jersey, coat

Materials: leather, nylon, fur, ivory, cotton, wool

Opinion adjectives: smart, nice, horrible, fashionable, unfashionable, attractive, cool, trendy

Physical appearance: smart, tidy, pretty, handsome, young, middle-aged, old, blonde, dark, tall, short, medium height, thin, slim, well-built, overweight, dark, fair

Opposites: conventional/unconventional; successful/unsuccessful; formal/informal; attractive/unattractive; legal/illegal

Verbs: try on, put on, look for, laugh at, stick up, go with

Shopping expressions: Can I help you? No thanks, I'm just looking. I'm looking for a skirt. What size are you? How much is this? That's too expensive. It's not big enough. That really suits you.

Module diary

- **Which was your favourite lesson in module 1? Why?**

  Example: Lesson 5, I enjoyed the fashion project.

- **Grade the reading texts in this module like this:**

  ☆☆☆ very difficult   ☆☆ OK   ☆ easy
  - Supermodel Celebrities   • the poem 'Alfie'
  - Fashion through the ages

- **Which was the most difficult part of the Final Writing Task?**

  a getting information

  b writing notes

  c writing the description

  d checking your partner's description

- **What was your score in the *Test Yourself* activity?**

- **Give yourself a mark for these structures:**
  - Basic tenses
  - Use of auxiliaries

  A I understand them very well.

  B I sometimes make mistakes.

  C I don't understand them.

MUSIC

Lead-in

Module Objectives   In this module you will ...

Read   about pop styles, guitar heroes and a violin virtuoso
Talk   about albums, rock stars and music you like
Listen   to different types of music, a song and a group
Practise   manager talking
using the past simple and past continuous and revise
conditional sentences

Your final tasks will be to write about a group and interview a rock star.

a

Look at the pictures and listen to the music. Guess which country each piece is from.

Example: 1 = Spain

b  KEYWORDS

Copy and complete the network with these words. Add more.

drums classical rap trumpet soul
blues violin reggae bass guitar
country and western keyboards

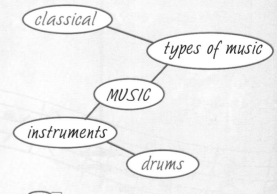

c

GUESS WHO?

In pairs, take turns to think of a singer, musician or group. Then ask questions to find out who it is.

Example: Is she from Europe?
Does he play the electric guitar?
Do they play rock music?

1

2

3

4

7 Pop Styles

A 📖

**Read the text quickly and match
the photos with a style of music.**

Pop Styles

🎵 **Blues** traditional black American music. 'Blue' means 'sad', and many blues songs are about how hard life was for black people.

🎵 **Gospel** religious music sung in churches in the southern USA.

🎵 **Rhythm and Blues** black workers in the USA moved from farms to the cities. They played the blues with electric guitars - this became 'rhythm and blues'.

🎵 **Country and Western** the music of poor white Americans in the 1930s and 1940s. It is still the most popular music in the southern USA.

🎵 **Rock 'n' Roll** many radio stations in the USA in the 1950s would not play 'black' music. Elvis Presley was one of the first white singers to mix 'rhythm and blues' and 'country and western'. The result was 'rock 'n' roll'.

🎵 **Soul** a mixture of 'gospel' and 'rhythm and blues'. The most successful soul singers are probably Stevie Wonder and Michael Jackson.

🎵 **Heavy Metal** a style based on 'rhythm and blues', but with the instruments amplified so they are extremely loud. Led Zeppelin was one of the first groups to do this.

🎵 **Reggae** this started in Jamaica. It is a mixture of African styles and 'rhythm and blues'. Bob Marley made it popular.

🎵 **Rap** in the 1980s, disc-jockeys in dance clubs began half singing and half talking over instrumental music – and 'rap' music was born.

🎵 **House** 1990s dance music based on very fast rhythms and modern electronic sounds. There are now various sub-styles of 'house music', such as 'techno pop', 'trance' and 'jungle'.

B

Read the text again and answer these questions.

1 What kind of music is gospel music?
2 Who started rhythm and blues music?
3 When did country and western music start?
4 Which two styles of music influenced rock 'n' roll?
5 Which style of music did Led Zeppelin develop?
6 Who made reggae music popular?
7 When did rap music originate?

C

Listen to some different styles of music. Try to match them with the styles described in the text.

D KEYWORDS

Complete these sentences with adjectives from the box.

> popular   poor   electric   successful   instrumental

1 Many people had no jobs and were very ... in the 1930s.
2 Heavy metal music is probably more ... with boys than girls.
3 ... music doesn't have any words or singing.
4 The Beatles were the most ... pop group of all time.
5 He plays his ... guitar really loud.

E   KEYWORDS

Copy the table and add the expressions to the correct columns.

> I don't mind it.   I love it.   I don't like it.
> I can't stand it.   I like it.   It's quite nice.
> I'm crazy about it.   It's OK.   It's horrible.
> It doesn't appeal to me.   It's all right.
> It's fantastic.   I hate it.

☆☆☆	☆	–	X	XXX
I love it.	I like it.	I don't mind it.	I don't like it.	I can't stand it.

F

Listen to the music in exercise C again. Write a sentence about each piece of music.

Example: House music doesn't appeal to me.

G

In groups, give your opinions about the music.

Example: A: I love reggae.
B: So do I.
C: I don't, I think it's horrible.

Report to the class the most popular kind of music in your group.

Did you know?

Oasis songs are heavily influenced by 1960s British pop, especially The Beatles.

25

8 Guitar Heroes

A

In pairs, list famous guitarists you like. Tell the class.

Example: We like Mark Knopfler from Dire Straits and Slash from Guns 'n' Roses.

B

Read about Jimi Hendrix and Bonnie Raitt. True or false?

1 Jimi Hendrix was popular in England before the USA.
2 Paul McCartney played the guitar with Jimi Hendrix.
3 Jimi's last successful album was a mixture of blues, classical and flamenco.
4 Bonnie Raitt came from a musical family.
5 A blues guitarist taught Bonnie how to play the guitar.
6 Bonnie didn't win a Grammy award.

Hendrix

Guitar Heroes

N° 16 **Jimi Hendrix**

Jimi Hendrix was born in Seattle in 1942. In the early 1960s he was a backing musician with soul and rock 'n' roll groups. An English musician saw him while he was playing in a club in 1966, and invited him to London. Jimi formed a group there and became popular. His music was a strange mixture of soul, blues, hard rock and even jazz. His first hit was the song 'Hey Joe'. While Jimi was working in a London club in 1967, Paul McCartney saw him and became one of his most famous fans. He played like no other guitarist – he even played solos with his teeth! At the time of his death he was planning a new album – a mixture of blues, classical and flamenco. He didn't make the album. He died of a drug overdose in 1970 while he was staying at a friend's house in London. However, we should remember him as a virtuoso musician of great quality.

Raitt

N° 47 **Bonnie Raitt**

Guitar Heroes

Bonnie Raitt was born in California in 1949. Her father was a singer and actor and her mother played the piano. As a child, while she was staying at a summer camp, she heard somebody playing folk music. She immediately taught herself to play the guitar and became interested in blues music. While at college, she protested against the Vietnam War. She played with blues groups in clubs and finally made her first album in 1971. Many famous musicians admired her unique guitar style. She had a great hit with her 1989 album called 'Nick of Time', which won a Grammy Award. When she isn't playing music, Bonnie fights for social causes – she is an environmentalist and has worked for Amnesty International.

Language Focus: Past simple/ past continuous

C

Are the verbs in italics in the past simple or past continuous tense?

Example: He *was playing* in a club in 1966.
(past continuous)
He even *played* solos with his teeth!
(past simple)

1 An English musician *saw* him while ...
2 Jimi *formed* a group ...
3 While Jimi *was working* ...
4 he *was planning* a new album ...
5 he *didn't make* the album ...
6 he *was staying* at a friend's house ...

Which of the verbs in the past simple are regular?

D

Which tense do we use:

1 to talk about an activity in the past?
2 to talk about a completed action in the past?

E

Put the verbs in brackets into the correct tense, past simple or past continuous.

Example: 1 = was

F 📼

Listen to the three guitar extracts and decide which is played in the style of – Jimi Hendrix, Bonnie Raitt and Django Reinhardt.

G

ROLE-PLAY

Imagine you are a great musician. Think about these things:

Where and when were you born?
Which instrument did you learn to play?
How did you learn to play it?
Who discovered you?
What were you doing at the time?
What did you do after that?
What are your plans for the future?

In pairs, take turns to interview your partner.

DJANGO REINHARDT

DJANGO REINHARDT [1] ... (be) born in 1910 into a Romany family who [2] ... (travel) in Belgium at the time. He [3] ... (teach) himself to play the guitar when he was twelve. As a teenager, he [4] ... (play) in clubs in Paris. At the age of eighteen, while he [5] ... (visit) his family, their caravan [6] ... (catch) fire. Django was badly burned and two fingers of his left hand [7] ... (be) paralysed. While he [8] ... (recuperate), he [9] ... (decide) to find a new way of playing the guitar with only two fingers. He [10] ... (develop) a new style and [11] ... (become) better than before! In the 1930s, while Django [12] ... (work) in a club in Paris, he [13] ... (meet) Stéphane Grappelli, a great violinist. Together, they [14] ... (form) a group. They [15] ... (make) an album, but the record company [16] ... (refuse) to release it because it was too 'modern'. Django [17] ... (die) in 1953, aged only 43, but his rich style proves he was a real virtuoso.

9 Virtuosos

A

Listen to three pieces of classical music. Choose from the words below to describe how each piece is played.

- slowly and sadly
- fast and spectacularly
- delicately and happily

B

Read the life story of Paganini. Which of the pieces of music in exercise A do you think he composed?

C

Read the text again and match these titles with the paragraphs.

- Lifestyle
- Childhood appearance
- Concerts
- Starting off

'If Paganini were alive today...'

Niccolò Paganini – the first pop star?

1 In 1782, Paganini was born into a poor Italian family. As a child, he looked *very* strange. He had a pale face and was *terribly* thin. He had bright eyes, long black hair and *incredibly* long fingers like bird claws.

2 One day, Niccolò discovered the violin. After that he practised *hard* every day, *rarely* stopping to eat or sleep. When he was nine he gave his first concert. He played *brilliantly* and everyone was *completely* amazed. Then at the age of fifteen he started planning his own tours. While he was touring, he wrote his famous Caprices.

3 His concerts were *highly* spectacular. He dressed in black and looked *really* sinister. *Sometimes*, while he was playing a difficult piece of music, he took out a pair of scissors, cut off three strings, and played the same piece on one string!

4 Paganini became as rich and famous as many modern pop stars. While he was touring Britain in 1831, he earned £16,000 – that's more than a quarter of a million pounds today! Crowds followed him in the street. He lived *extravagantly*, becoming a passionate gambler and having love affairs all over Europe. At the height of his fame, he stopped playing the violin and taught himself to play the guitar. Nobody ever heard him play it, but he wrote some *extremely* difficult pieces of music. When he died, in 1840, his violin was placed in the City Hall of Genoa, and is known as 'Paganini's widow'. *Occasionally* it is played by a visiting virtuoso.

D

Are these sentences true or false?

1 Paganini came from a rich family.
2 He was living at home when he wrote his 'Caprices'.
3 His concerts were exciting to watch.
4 He earned £16,000 in 1831 while he was touring Italy.

E

Copy the table. Now put the adverbs in italics from the text opposite into the correct groups.

How something is done	hard
How often something is done	rarely
With an adjective or another adverb	very strange

F

Choose the correct adverb to complete the text.

MOZART came from a ¹ (very/always) musical family. He could play the harpsichord ² (hard/ brilliantly) at the age of three! From the age of five he was writing ³ (sometimes/ extremely) difficult pieces of music, and by the time he was eight he had become ⁴ (rarely/incredibly) popular all over Europe. He had a strange lifestyle, though – he ⁵ (really/rarely) slept in the same bed for more than three nights. He wrote some ⁶ (highly/ strongly) successful operas, but ⁷ (never/ occasionally) became rich.

G

Listen to Andy and Jan talking about going to a concert.

1 Who suggests going out?
2 Can the other person go?
3 Where do they agree to go? When?

H

ROLE-PLAY

In pairs, follow the instructions below and act out a dialogue like the one in exercise G.

A

Say hello.

You can't. Say why not. Suggest another night or another concert.

Agree. Suggest a time and place to meet.

Say goodbye.

B

Say hello. Invite him/her to go and see a local group tonight. Say what music they play.

You can't. Say why not. Suggest doing something different next week.

Agree. Say goodbye.

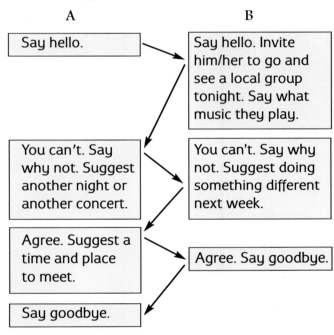

Did you know?

Paganini was the fastest violinist in the world. He could play twelve notes per second!

10 Albums

A

In groups, discuss the questions below:

1 What do you think are best: records, cassettes or compact discs?
2 What is the name of your favourite album? Who is it by?

B

Listen to a manager talking about making an album.
Put the photos in the correct order.

C

Listen again. Copy and complete the sentences in the box.

CONDITIONAL TYPE 1

If you prepare well, the recording ... a success.
If the fans have a good time at your concert, they ... the album!

CONDITIONAL TYPE 2

If we had more money, we ... more time in the studio.
If nobody bought them, it ... a disaster.

D

Which type of conditional sentence do we use:

1 to talk about imaginary situations?
2 to talk about real future situations?

E

Copy and complete this table with the tenses used for conditional sentences.

	CONDITION	CONSEQUENCE
Type I	*if + present simple*	.....
Type 2	*if + ...*	*conditional (would)*

F

Match the two parts to make complete sentences.

Example: 1 = c

1 If he had enough money,
2 If you touched this key,
3 If you practised more,
4 If you play it louder,
5 If you listen to very loud music,
6 If you want to be a virtuoso,

a the keyboard would make this sound.
b you will hurt your ears.
c he would buy an electric guitar.
d you won't be able to hear me sing!
e you will have to practise every day.
f you would play better.

G DICTIONARY SKILLS

The underlined words have more than one meaning. Look them up in the mini-dictionary and write the number of the appropriate meaning.

1 I like your outfit. You look really <u>cool</u>.
2 I've got a <u>rough</u> idea for a song but I haven't finished it yet.
3 Reggae is based on African <u>styles</u> of music.
4 I don't like my brother's <u>taste</u> in music.
5 He <u>treated</u> his guitar very roughly and now it's broken.

H

Read the questionnaire and think about your answers. Then, in pairs, tell your partner about yourself.

Example: A: I can't play anything. What about you?
B: I can play the piano.

The Music Questionnaire

1 **Can you play a musical instrument? If so, which one?**

2 **If you could choose any instrument, which one would you like to play really well?**

3 **If your parents had a party, what kind of music would they play?**

4 **When you go to a party, what kind of music do you play?**

5 **Will you buy a new album if you go shopping this weekend?**

6 **If you could take only three albums with you to a desert island, which three would you take?**

7 **Have you ever been to a music concert? If so, who did you see?**

8 **If you could see any group or singer you wanted, who would you see?**

9 **Who is your favourite rock star? If you met him/her, what would you say or do?**

10 **If you have children when you're older, do you think they will like your music?**

11 Fluency

A

In pairs, find out which of these things your partner does when he/she listens to pop songs in English.

a listens to the songs and tries to understand a few words

b listens to the songs but does not worry about the words

c listens to the songs and tries to write down the words, stopping the cassette and rewinding

d looks at a copy of the words and tries to translate them

B

Listen to the Eurythmics song and complete the text below.

Who's That Girl?

The language of love
Slips from my lover's tongue
Cooler than ^{1} ...
And warmer than the ^{2} ...
Dumb hearts get broken
Just like China cups
The language of love
Has left me ^{3} ... on the rocks.

But there's just one thing
Just one thing
But there's just one thing
And I really wanna know.

Who's that girl
^{4} ... around with you?
Tell me.

The language of love
Has ^{5} ... me stony grey
Tongue-tied and twisted
At the price I've had to ^{6} ...
Your careless notions
Have silenced these ^{7} ...
Look at all the foolishness
Your lover's ^{8} ... has done.

(words and music by
Annie Lennox and Dave Stewart)

C

In pairs, discuss your answers to the questionnaire below.

BODY LANGUAGE QUESTIONNAIRE

1 What do you do when you meet someone you don't know?
a) Shake hands with the person.
b) Kiss the person once or twice?
c) Speak but don't touch.

2 Which of the above do you do when you meet a friend in the street?

3 When someone is relaxed and friendly to you, which of these things do they do?
a) Fold their arms and cross their legs.
b) Look at you and smile.
c) Stand quite close to you.
d) Avoid looking at you.
e) Stand a long way from you.

Final Writing Task: A Profile

D

Invent a rock group and write a profile of them.

Stage 1 Planning: In groups, share your ideas and make notes. Decide on these things:

BACKGROUND INFORMATION
- name of the group – The Benefits
- style of music they play – hard rock
- members of the group (one name for each student in the group) – Rono, Deke Roberts, ...
- instruments they play – guitars, drums, ...

EARLY DAYS
- how they met – at school
- first concert – at a club in London, only six people came!
- first time in the studio – after they met their manager, only had two hours' studio time!
- first album and the titles of a few songs – 'House of Sleep' ...

FUTURE PLANS
- what they are doing now – writing music for a film ...
- plans for the future – an American tour next year, a new video, ...

Stage 2 Writing: Use your notes to write three paragraphs about the group you have invented. Use linking words (*when, after that,* etc.)

Stage 3 Checking: Check your writing for spelling and punctuation.

Final Speaking Task: An Interview

E

In pairs, interview a rock star.

- One student is a rock star – a member of the group you invented in exercise D.
- The other is a journalist and interviews the star.

Example:
A: How did you meet the other members of the group?
B: Well, we were all at the same school. I met Rono first – we were having a fight about a girlfriend!
A: When was your first concert?
B: I remember that very well. We played at a club in London. It was a disaster, because only about six people came ...

Did you know?
A 15-year-old drummer called Larry Mullen put a note on his school noticeboard in Dublin to see if anybody was interested in forming a group. They were ~ and that group became U2!

33

12 Consolidation

Grammar

A

Complete the text with the verbs in brackets in the past simple or past continuous.

Example: 1 = were attending

U2 Factfile

All four members of the group ¹ … (attend) the same school in Dublin in 1977 when they ² … (form) the group. They ³ … (win) a music competition at school.

U2 ⁴ … (take) their name from an American spy aeroplane which the Russians ⁵ … (shoot) down during the early 60s while it ⁶ … (fly) over Moscow.

While they ⁷ … (tour) in the USA, bass guitarist Andy Clayton ⁸ … (meet) top model Naomi Campbell. They ⁹ … (plan) to marry, but in the end they didn't.

In 1992, the UK government ¹⁰ … (have) plans to extend a nuclear power station – U2 ¹¹ … (organise) a demonstration against it and ¹² … (play) a concert for Greenpeace in Manchester.

President Clinton once ¹³ … (phone) the group while they ¹⁴ … (give) an interview on live TV in New York!

Bono ¹⁵ … (be) mistaken for a drugs dealer in 1996! While his private plane ¹⁶ … (land) in Jamaica, the police ¹⁷ … (shoot) at him.

While they ¹⁸ … (record) their album *Pop*, a computer hacker ¹⁹ … (steal) the songs, which ²⁰ … (delay) the album.

In September 1997 they ²¹ … (play) the first rock concert in Sarajevo after the war there to a multi-ethnic audience.

B

Complete the sentences with the verbs in the correct tense.

1 If U2 were on tour in her town, she … (go) to see them.
2 If I see John, I … (ask) him about the concert.
3 If I had one of Jimi Hendrix's guitars, I … (not sell) it.
4 If I could play the guitar, I … (like) to play like Eric Clapton.
5 If that song comes on the radio, I … (record) it for you.
6 If she heard soul music, she … (start) dancing.
7 If I win a lot of money, I … (buy) a recording studio.

Vocabulary

C 🔑 KEYWORDS

Complete the sentences with these words.

> guitar solo   group   styles   album   fan
> hit   mixture   tour   backing musician

1 He started as a … with a local … .
2 He plays a strange … of … .
3 He sometimes plays a long … .
4 He is going on a … of the USA.
5 I'm a great … of his.
6 I think his next … will be a big … .

D 🔑 KEYWORDS

Match words from each column to make styles of music.

1	rock 'n'	a	blues
2	heavy	b	pop
3	rhythm and	c	rock
4	hard	d	roll
5	country and	e	western
6	techno	f	metal

E KEYWORDS

Make adjectives from these nouns.

Example: sadness (*n*) – sad (*adj*)

> sadness   tradition   success   music
> popularity   poverty

Pronunciation

F KEYWORDS

Copy the table on the right and put these words in the correct column according to their stress pattern.

> successful   saxophone   trumpet
> keyboards   extremely   classical   completely
> instrument   reggae   musician   popular
> piano   musical   gospel

1 □■□	**2** ■□□	**3** ■□
successful	saxophone	trumpet

Now listen, check your answers and repeat the words.

G

Listen to the first sound in these three words.

Group 1	Group 2	Group 3
/w/ would	/k/ could	/g/ good

Listen to five sentences which start with these words. Which sentences are incorrect? Now listen to five more sentences and repeat them.

Test Yourself

A (10 points)

Complete the text with the verbs in the past simple or past continuous.

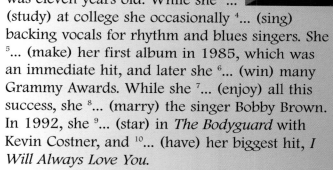

Whitney Houston was born into a musical family in Newark, New Jersey, in 1963. Her mother, Cissy Houston, was a gospel music singer and sometimes ¹... (perform) as a backing vocalist with Elvis Presley. Whitney ²... (begin) singing gospel songs in church when she was eleven years old. While she ³... (study) at college she occasionally ⁴... (sing) backing vocals for rhythm and blues singers. She ⁵... (make) her first album in 1985, which was an immediate hit, and later she ⁶... (win) many Grammy Awards. While she ⁷... (enjoy) all this success, she ⁸... (marry) the singer Bobby Brown. In 1992, she ⁹... (star) in *The Bodyguard* with Kevin Costner, and ¹⁰... (have) her biggest hit, *I Will Always Love You.*

B (5 points)

Complete the sentences with the correct form of the verb in brackets.

1 If I go near the theatre, I ... (see) what time the concert starts.
2 If I ... (not have) any homework, I will play my electric guitar.
3 If they ... (have) a contract, they would make an album.
4 If she goes to a party, she ... (take) some 'house' music.
5 If he practised more, he ... (pass) the piano exam.

Extra Time

Look at Reading Club 2 on page 97.

Module Check

Language Check

PAST SIMPLE
Paganini **played** the violin.
They **made** an album.
He **didn't play** hard rock.
When **did** they **make** that album?

PAST CONTINUOUS
He **was living** in Belgium.
They **were playing** in a club.
She **wasn't feeling** very happy.
We **weren't touring** at the time.
Was he **listening** to his cassettes?
Were you **making** a lot of money?

CONDITIONAL SENTENCES
If the album **sells**, we'**ll make** a lot of money.
(Type 1)
If they **had** more money, they **would spend** more time in the studio. (Type 2)

Keyword Check

- **Make sure you know the meaning of these words and expressions.**
- **Put important new words in your vocabulary book.**

General: group, hit, fan, solo, album, tour, backing musician
Instruments: drums, guitar, keyboard, violin, bass guitar
Styles: classical, rap, blues, rock 'n' roll, rhythm and blues, country and western
Nouns and adjectives: tradition/traditional, popularity/popular, success/successful, poverty/poor, music/musical
Adverbs of manner: brilliantly, extravagantly, well, hard, spectacularly
Adverbs of frequency: often, sometimes, rarely, occasionally
Adverbs of degree: incredibly, completely, really, extremely
Expressing likes and dislikes: I love it. I don't mind it. I can't stand it.

- **Try to add more words to each list.**

Module diary

- **Which was your favourite lesson in module 2? Why?**
  Example: Guitar Heroes, because I am learning to play the guitar.
- **Write down something interesting or unusual from the module.**
  Example: Paganini could play twelve notes per second.
- **Which of the listenings was most difficult?**
  - the manager's advice
  - going to a concert
  - the song

What was your score in the *Test Yourself* activity?
- **Give yourself a mark for these structures:**
  - Past simple/past continuous
  - Conditional sentences
  A I understand them very well.
  B I sometimes make mistakes.
  C I don't understand them.
- **Assess your speaking this term:**
  A I try to speak English all the time in class.
  B I participate quite well in pair/group activities.
  C I should try to speak English more in class.

HOLIDAYS
Lead-in

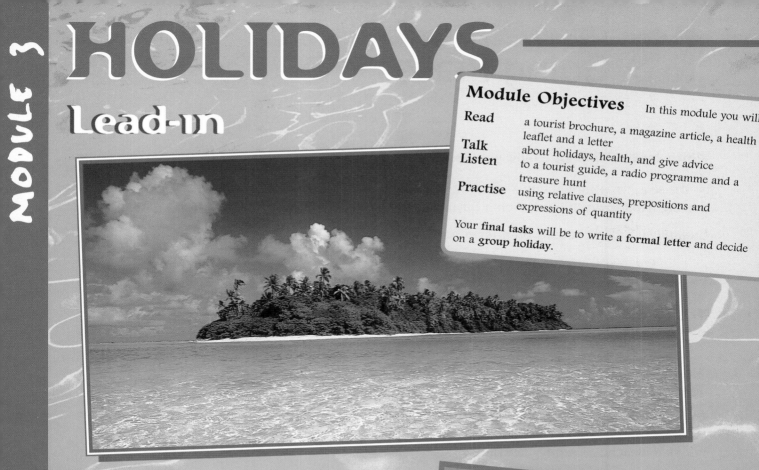

Module Objectives   In this module you will ...

Read   a tourist brochure, a magazine article, a health leaflet and a letter

Talk   about holidays, health, and give advice
Listen   to a tourist guide, a radio programme and a treasure hunt

Practise   using relative clauses, prepositions and expressions of quantity

Your **final tasks** will be to write a **formal letter** and decide on a **group holiday**.

a KEYWORDS

Look at the words in the box. Which things can you see in the photos?

> hotel island tourist sandy beach
> restaurant swimming pool museum
> blue sky monument clean sea deck chair

b

In pairs, tell your partner about a good holiday you have had.

Example: I once went to Paris.
   I saw the . . .

13 Going Places

A

Which type of holiday would you prefer? Tell the class.

by the sea / in a capital city / camping / on an island /
touring from town to town / on a farm

Example: I'd like a holiday on a farm because I love animals.

B  KEYWORDS

**Match the words in the box with the topics in the table
in exercise C.**

> sunny windsurfing friendly sandy facilities delicacy
> Roman ruins deserted 5-star skiing hospitable
> breezes rocky seafood sailing luxury castle

Example: Beaches – sandy, deserted, rocky

C

**Read the brochure about Barbados. Copy and complete
the table with information from the brochure.**

BEACHES	30 miles white sand
WEATHER	
SPORTS	
EXCURSIONS	
PEOPLE	
HOTELS	
FOOD	

D

**Listen to the dialogue and check the information with the
brochure. Find five mistakes that the new travel agent
makes.**

Example: *Travel agent:* it's always very hot
        Brochure: fresh island breezes keep us cool

BAR

Welcome to beautiful Barbados. This is the island where the sun shines for over 3,000 hours a year, and where we have fresh island breezes to keep us cool. We have more than thirty miles of white sandy beaches and clear blue waters. In Barbados you can relax and forget the stress and worries of the rest of the world.

There is lots to do for everyone. There are ideal conditions for swimming on the west coast, and for windsurfing and surfing on the south coast. There are also many interesting places to visit on the island. You can go on excursions like the cruise on the *Jolly Roger*, which is a famous pirate ship.

The Barbadians are people who are friendly, fun-loving and hospitable. We have a distinctive culture, with African roots and an important British influence. We can also be proud of our country, which has a literacy rate of over 95% and over 350 years of democratic government.

There is a wide choice of hotel accommodation, from luxury hotels to modest, comfortable guest houses for you to stay in. And you must try some of our fantastic food that includes exotic delicacies such as lobster and flying fish.

BADOS

Language Focus: Relative clauses

E

Match the sentence halves to make complete sentences.

Example: 1 = c

1 This is the island
2 You can go on a cruise on the Jolly Roger
3 The Barbadians are people
4 We are proud of our country
5 You must try some of our fantastic food

a that includes lobster and flying fish.
b who are friendly, fun-loving and hospitable.
c where the sun shines for over 3,000 hours a year.
d which is a famous pirate ship.
e which has a literacy rate of over 95%.

F

Complete the definitions with *who*, *which* or *where*.

Example: 1 = where

1 A wildlife reserve is a place ... wild animals live and are protected.
2 An island is a piece of land ... is surrounded by water.
3 A tourist is a person ... travels for pleasure.
4 A breeze is a wind ... is very light.
5 A beach is a place next to the sea ... you can swim.
6 A travel agent is a person ... helps people to arrange their holidays.

G KEYWORDS

Choose a holiday destination (real or imaginary). Think of adjectives and write notes using the headings in exercise C, like this:

> **Place:** Crete
> **Beaches:** fantastic/sandy
> **Weather:** beautiful – warm and sunny from May to October
> **People:** very friendly/a lot of people speak English
> **Food:** delicious traditional Greek dishes

H

HOLIDAY GAME

In pairs, ask ten yes/no questions about your partner's holiday from exercise G. You get one point for every 'yes' answer.

Example: A: Is the weather hot?
B: Yes. (1 point)
A: Do the people speak English?
B: No. (0 points)

14 Exploring Barbados

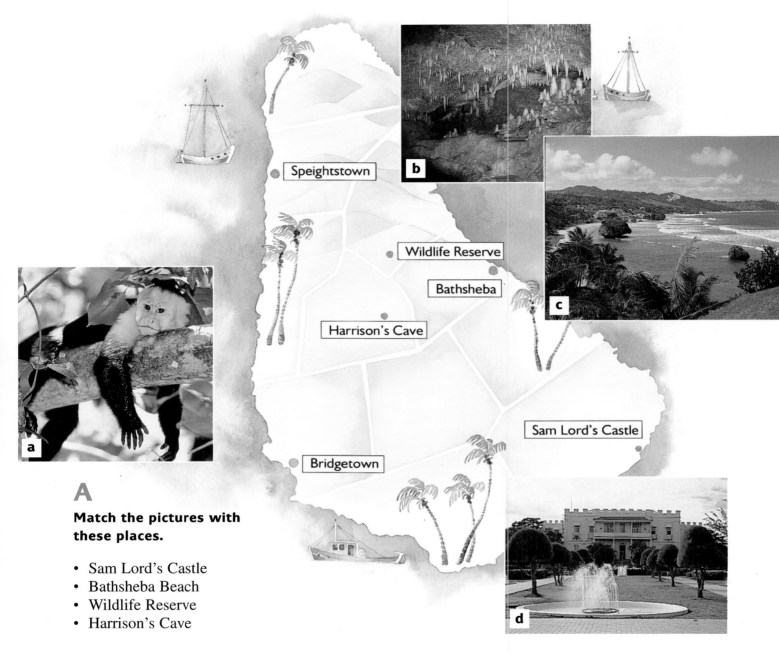

Speightstown

Wildlife Reserve

Bathsheba

Harrison's Cave

Sam Lord's Castle

Bridgetown

A

Match the pictures with these places.

- Sam Lord's Castle
- Bathsheba Beach
- Wildlife Reserve
- Harrison's Cave

B

Listen to the guide and the two tourists. Choose the correct answer.

1 In Speightstown you can see
   a old ships.   **b** old cars.   **c** old forts.
2 In the Wildlife Reserve there are rare
   a tortoises.   **b** monkeys.   **c** peacocks.
3 Tours of Harrison's Cave last
   a an hour.   **b** half an hour.   **c** two hours.
4 The sea at Bathsheba Beach has dangerous
   a fish.   **b** sand.   **c** currents.
5 They say there's hidden treasure at Sam Lord's Castle in the
   a pool.   **b** gardens.   **c** cave.

Which place on the island would you like to visit?

Language Focus: Preposition review

C

Use these prepositions to complete the text below. Then listen and check your answers.

up / along (x2) / through / at / out / in / to / down / with / about / on / of

Example: 1 = through

Well, you go ¹ ... Bridgetown and then go ² ... the coast. If you are interested ³ ... old buildings, you can visit the old forts in Speightstown. Now, when you drive ⁴ ... of Speightstown you'll go ⁵ ... a hill. Then, as you come ⁶ ... it, you'll see the Barbados Wildlife Reserve on the left. If you're keen ⁷ ... wildlife, it's really worth visiting.
You go ⁸ ... the Bridgetown road until you arrive ⁹ ... Harrison's Cave. Don't be frightened ¹⁰ ... visiting it.
If you're bored ¹¹ ... sightseeing, you can go ¹² ... the beach at Bathsheba and have a picnic. But be careful ¹³ ... swimming in the sea.

D

Find examples in exercise C of:

1 verbs with prepositions (e.g. *go through*)
2 adjectives with prepositions (e.g. *interested in*)

Add other examples to the lists if you can.

E

PRONUNCIATION

Listen to the sentences and mark the stressed words.

Example: 1 Go □ through the town and turn □ left □
□ □
next to the football ground.

1 Go through the town and turn left next to the football ground.
2 You go up the hill and you'll see the house on the right.
3 Go along the Bridgetown road until you arrive at the cave.
4 Go under the bridge and the castle is opposite the church.
5 Go past the cinema and it's the third on the right.

In pairs practise saying the sentences with the correct stress.

F

In pairs, think of an interesting place to visit in your area.

Examples: a historic building / a beach / a nature reserve

Write about the place and how to get there, like this:

If you are interested in castles, you can visit Ludlow where there is a fantastic castle. Go out of Leominster and take the Shrewsbury road. After twelve kilometres you will see a turning for Ludlow on the left. Go into the centre of the town and you will see the castle which is next to the river. The castle is very large and from the top of it you can see for miles.

G

In groups, read out your suggestions. Decide on the most popular place to visit.

Action Holidays

ACTION HOLIDAYS IN RUSSIA

A re you looking for some action? Sally Parker spoke to several young people who had been to Russia.

Sue and Neil went to Siberia for their honeymoon! 'It was really fantastic,' said Neil. 'We spent most of the time sailing on Lake Baikal where there were lovely sandy beaches and some beautiful islands. You don't have to know how to sail – there are guides – but really, you ought to have lessons. Sailing's great fun.' Sue agreed, 'Yes, it was lovely. We also did some horseriding and finally flew in a helicopter above the Siberian forests. If you ever do that, you'd better take some warm clothes – it was absolutely freezing!'

Maria and Daniel are both 19 and went skiing in the Caucasus mountains. Mount Elbrus, which is 5642 m, is one of the highest mountains in Europe.

'Before you go up though', laughed Daniel, 'it's a good idea to check the distance as well as the difficulty of the descent. We had a great time, though, skiing and relaxing.'

Martin, who is 35, chose Kamchatka, one of the wildest places in eastern Russia. 'We had nine days of rafting and fishing along the Bystraya river. Marvellous. Then the hard bit – climbing the Mutnovsky volcano. You shouldn't choose this type of holiday if you like crowded discotheques or swimming pools. We didn't meet anybody – although we did see a few brown Kamchatski bears!'

George and Hamish went paragliding in the Caucasus. This holiday is only for experienced paragliders with an international certificate or pilot's card. You should also have some insurance.

For more information about action holidays in Russia, phone Russotours 010 249 3481 for a free brochure.

A

Which of these holiday activities appeal to you? Tell the class.

rafting / sailing / horseriding / climbing / paragliding / skiing / fishing

Example: I'd really like to try paragliding.

B

Read the text quickly. In which paragraphs are the activities in exercise A mentioned?

C

Which of these statements are facts and which are opinions?

1 Most of Sue and Neil's holiday was spent sailing.
2 Neil thinks sailing is great fun.
3 It's very cold above the Siberian forest.
4 Mount Elbrus is the highest mountain in Europe.
5 Rafting and fishing in Kamchatka is a marvellous experience.
6 You need a pilot's card to go on this paragliding holiday.

D
 KEYWORDS

Read the text again and complete the advice with the expressions in the box.

> ought   a good idea   should   don't have
> (had)'d better   shouldn't

1 You ... to know how to sail.
2 You ... to have lessons.
3 You ... take some warm clothes.
4 It's ... to check the distance.
5 You ... choose this type of holiday.
6 You ... have some insurance.

E

Plan an action holiday, real or imaginary. Make notes about these things:

GEOGRAPHY	lake, mountains, town, sea, river, forest
DURATION	a week, ten days, three weeks
ACTIVITIES	fishing, horseriding, swimming
ADVICE	you should ..., it's a good idea to ..., you don't have to ...

F

In groups, take turns to talk about your action holiday. Then decide which one sounds the most interesting.

G
 LONGMAN DICTIONARY SKILLS

Singular or plural? Definite or indefinite article or no article? Use the mini-dictionary and complete the sentences.

1 If you don't put a coat on when you go out, you'll get ... cold and you'll have to stay in bed.
2 His concerts were all ... great successes.
3 It was ... stress of her new job that made her ill.
4 I must get ... new string for my guitar.
5 Learning English helps ... communication between people from different countries.
6 They are going to wear ... formal dress for the wedding.

16 The Dark Side of the Sun

A

In groups, decide which of these holiday activities is the most dangerous. Then tell the class what could go wrong.

mountain climbing / swimming / sunbathing / skiing / playing ball games on the beach

Example: We think mountain climbing is the most dangerous; you could fall and hurt yourself or even die.

B 📖

Read the extract from a health shop leaflet and find out which activity is the most dangerous.

Sun friend or foe?

Nowadays, everybody is aware of the importance of a healthy life. We know all about healthy eating, healthy drinking, exercise and looking good. And after our holidays it's nice to go back to work or school with a 'healthy' suntan. But is it? Scientists now believe that of all holiday activities, sunbathing is the most dangerous to our health.

C

Listen to the first part of the holiday programme. Copy and complete the table.

THE SUN'S RADIATION	EFFECTS
Ultra-violet A	
Ultra-violet B	
Ultra-violet C	can cause skin cancer and …

Language focus: Quantity

D

Listen to the second part of the holiday programme to complete these sentences.

INTERVIEWER: How can we protect ourselves? With ¹ ... protection cream?

WOMAN: No, you need to use ² ... sun protection cream. But be careful, ³ ... creams only protect you from ultra-violet B rays, and they provide ⁴ ... protection against the other rays from the sun.

INTERVIEWER: And ⁵ ... time do you recommend sunbathing? ⁶ ... hours a day?

WOMAN: Well, if you mean lying in the sun, then ⁷ ... . ⁸ ... sun is bad for you. Only ⁹ ... minutes on the first day. ¹⁰ ... people return from their holiday with their skin completely ruined.

E

Copy and complete the table with expressions of quantity from the interview. Which can we use with countable nouns, uncountable nouns or both?

COUNTABLE	UNCOUNTABLE	BOTH
a few	a lot of	plenty of

F

Choose five items from the list below and write how much you eat, drink or do.

Example: I eat hardly any meat. I drink too much lemonade! I walk a lot.

meat / fish / pasta / rice / sweets / lemonade / milk / fruit / chocolate / walk / travel by car / swim / sunbathe

G

In groups of four, choose three items from exercise F and find out how healthy the other students are.

Example: A: How many sweets do you eat?
B: None.
C: A lot.
D: Hardly any.

H

Tell the class about one person in your group.

Example: I think Eva is healthy because she hardly ever sunbathes, she eats plenty of fruit and she drinks a lot of milk.

Did you know?

In 1 second the Sun emits 35 million times the average annual electricity supply for the USA.

17 Fluency

Final Speaking Task: Choosing A Holiday

A

- **Look at the list of holidays and put them in order of preference.**

  ~ a visit to London, staying in a 5-star hotel
  ~ a camping holiday on the coast of France
  ~ an action holiday in Russia
  ~ a beach holiday in the Canaries, staying in an apartment
  ~ touring by car and caravan in Scotland

- **In groups, take turns to talk about your preferences and try to persuade the others to go on holiday with you for a week.**

  Example: I think we should go to London. There are lots of things to do and see. For example, ...

- **Try to agree on the most popular holiday. Then tell the class.**

Final Writing Task: A Formal Letter

B

Read the letter to a holiday company. What is wrong with it? Replace the words numbered with the words and expressions below:

arriving / would like / reserve / requested / Yours sincerely / confirm the reservation / thank you / enclosed / leaving / arrange this / I look forward to hearing from you

Example: Thanks = Thank you

Avenida Florida, 27
08024 Barcelona
Spain

5th May, 1999
UK Breaks
London SW12 6PN

Dear Sir/Madam,

¹ Thanks for the brochure. I ² want to arrange an action holiday with your company.

I would like to ³ get an apartment for four people (one bedroom plus a sofa-bed) in Newquay. We are ⁴ coming on Saturday, 12th July and are ⁵ going home on 19th July. We would like windsurfing and scuba diving classes. I have ⁶ put in a cheque for a deposit of £100, as you ⁷ asked.

I would also like to rent a car for the week. Could your company ⁸ sort this out? Please let me know what documents you need when you ⁹ tell me everything's OK.

¹⁰ Write soon,

¹¹ All the best,

Mario Delgado

C

Write a letter to a holiday company asking them to arrange a holiday for you.

Stage 1: Planning Decide on this information:
~ what type of holiday
~ number of people
~ dates
~ requirements (accommodation, classes, car, etc.).

Stage 2: Writing Write your letter. Make sure you:
~ set it out correctly (addresses, etc.)
~ use formal words and expressions.

Stage 3: Checking Give your letter to your partner to check. Change anything that is too personal or informal.

Stage 4: Feedback In groups, read each other's letters. Decide which is the best and read it out to the class.

D

Look at the picture of a Barbadian mansion and listen to the directions. Where in the garden is the treasure buried?

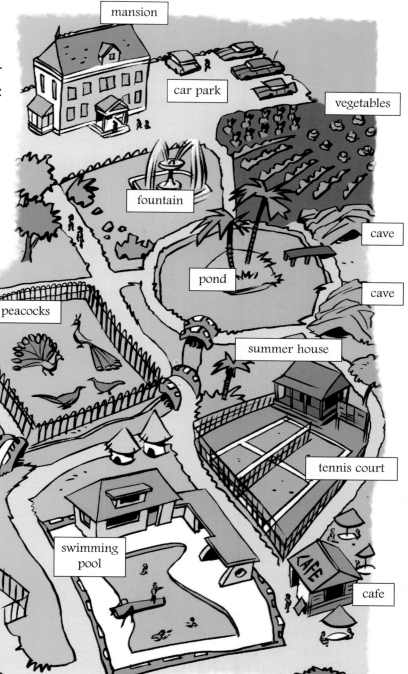

18 Consolidation

Grammar

A

Complete the text below with *who*, *which* or *where*.

We were planning our holiday. I phoned my cousin, Jenny, ¹... works in a travel agency. I said, "We want to spend a week in a place ²... there is plenty of sunshine. We'd like a town on the coast ³... we can swim, but we don't want anywhere ⁴... is very noisy. My mother, ⁵... has not been well this year, needs somewhere quiet. Can you recommend a suitable holiday place ⁶... is not very expensive?"

B

Read the text and choose the correct preposition.

Example: 1 = along

We drove ¹ (next to/along) the coast and arrived ² (at/to) the hotel about midday. Our room was ³ (in/on) the third floor, with a beautiful view ⁴ (for/of) the sea. After unpacking, we went ⁵ (below/down) to the hotel pool, and then had a meal ⁶ (at/of) the bar, which was just ⁷ (next to/at) the pool.

C

Complete the text with these words:

any / lot / plenty / few / too / some / much

Example: 1 = lot

In a ¹... of summer schools, you just do a ²... English lessons in the morning, and there's not ³... to do the rest of the day. Last year though, I went to a summer school in Ireland. We had ⁴... lessons each morning, and then there were ⁵... of activities organised by the teachers, such as tennis, football and swimming. The best thing was that we didn't get ⁶... much homework, and there weren't ⁷... exams at the end of the course!

Vocabulary

D KEYWORDS

Complete the sentences with the words in the box.

interested keen famous bored fond

1 I'm not very ... on action holidays.
2 Barbados is ... for its beautiful beaches.
3 He's quite ... of seafood.
4 I get ... with visiting museums.
5 She's very ... in architecture.

E  KEYWORDS

Make a new word from the word in brackets to complete the sentences.

1 Barbados has got lovely ... beaches. (*sand*)
2 We had a really ... holiday. (*relaxation*)
3 The people were very ... . (*friend*)
4 We stayed in a ... hotel. (*comfort*)
5 The beaches weren't very ... . (*crowd*)

F

ADJECTIVE GAME

In pairs, take turns to say an adjective to describe the things below. If you can't think of an adjective, you are out of the game and your partner gets a point.

beach / holiday / hotel / local people

Example: A: a crowded beach
B: a clean beach
A: a dirty beach
B: a sandy beach
A: Er, er ... (out of the game)

Pronunciation

G

Look at the list of the most common pronunciation problems. Which of them do you have?

1 Making mistakes with vowel sounds (e.g. live /ɪ/, leave /iː/).
2 Pronouncing words with lots of consonants together (e.g. *straight*).
3 Getting the stress in words wrong (e.g. saying comfort'able not 'comfortable).
4 Forgetting the endings of words (plurals/*ed*).
5 Pronouncing letters when they should be silent (e.g. 'ɪslənd / 'aɪlənd/)

Listen to a student talking about himself and his family. Write down the words he does not pronounce correctly and the number of the problem from the list above.

Example: description = 2

Test Yourself

A (10 points)

Robinson Crusoe's island holiday lasted longer than he expected! Complete the story with these prepositions:

back / across / up / under / into (x2) / from / at / along / to

Robinson Crusoe

was a sailor from Britain whose ship sank. He swam [1] ... the coast of a small, deserted island. The first night he was frightened, so he climbed [2] ... to the top of a tree to sleep. In the next few days he rescued some important things [3] ... the ship, which was near the coast. After that he put up his tent [4] ... a big tree. Then he explored the island. He walked [5] ... the coast and also went [6] ... the jungle. Next he went [7] ... the island to the other side. While he was on the island he did lots of things. He built a house, collected fruit and hunted wild goats. He also made a canoe, but he couldn't get it [8] ... the water. In the end a ship stopped [9] ... the island and took him [10] ... to Britain.

B (5 points)

Complete the dialogue with one suitable word in each gap.

A: How [1] ... money have we got?
B: Well, we've got [2] ... , but not a [3] ... .
A: How about going away for a [4] ... days next month?
B: Okay, I'll send for [5] ... brochures.

Extra Time

Look at Reading Club 3 on page 98.

49

Module Check

Language Check

PREPOSITIONS WITH VERBS

Go along the coast.
The restaurant **was next to** the pool.
We **arrived at** the hotel.

PREPOSITIONS WITH ADJECTIVES

I'm **bored with** all those museum visits.
He's **keen on** scuba diving.
Burgos is **famous for** its cathedral.

QUANTITY

Use **plenty** of sun protection cream.
Too much sun is bad for your skin.
Only spend **a few** minutes in the sun on your first day.

RELATIVE CLAUSES/PRONOUNS

People: She was the guide **who** took us to the cave. It was my brother **that** chose this holiday.
Things: This is a cream **which** protects you from Ultra-violet B rays. Paragliding is a sport **that** I don't want to try.
Places: It's the river **where** you can go rafting. It's the beach **that** we always go to in the summer.

Keyword Check

- **Make sure you know the meaning of these words and expressions.**
- **Put important new words in your vocabulary book.**

Weather: sunny, breeze, freezing
Activities: windsurfing, rafting, sunbathing, paragliding
Places: castle, ruins, beach, mountain, lake
Expressions: interested in, keen on, frightened of, famous for, bored with, fond of
Adjectives: sandy, relaxing, friendly, exotic, comfortable
Directions: go through, go along, go past, go under
Advice: You should take some warm clothes. You ought to reserve a room. You don't have to know how to sail.

- **Try to add more words to each list.**

Module diary

- **Which was your favourite lesson in module 3? Why?**
  Example: The lesson on action holidays because I'd like to go too.
- **Write down something interesting or unusual from this module.**
  Example: I didn't know the sun was so bad for your skin.
- **What was your score in the *Test Yourself* activity?**
- **Give yourself a mark for these structures:**
  - Prepositions
  - Quantity words
  - Relative clauses / pronouns

A I understand them.
B I sometimes make mistakes.
C I don't understand them.

- **Which of these things do you do when writing a composition?**
  always make a plan / check for mistakes / re-write / try to link sentences and ideas / use the new grammar I've studied / look at mistakes I've made in previous pieces of writing and try not to make them again
- **Look at your vocabulary book. How do you organise it?**
  alphabetically / for each module / with translations / with example sentences

SCIENCE

Lead-in

a 📖

In pairs, read these sentences.
Decide if the information is true or false.

A very fast computer can perform over 130 billion instructions per second!

Some silicon chips are less than 1 mm wide.

Nuclear power stations split atoms to produce heat and then electricity.

Lasers are used in eye surgery and can remove cancer cells.

NMR (nuclear magnetic resonance) scans can give us a picture of inside a body.

Check your answers on page 95.

Module Objectives
In this module you will ...

Read	about computers, women scientists and modern medicine
Talk	about inventions and discoveries
Listen	to a science quiz and a TV documentary
Practise	using passives and *still*, *yet* and *already*

Your **final tasks** will be to write a **report** and do a **survey**.

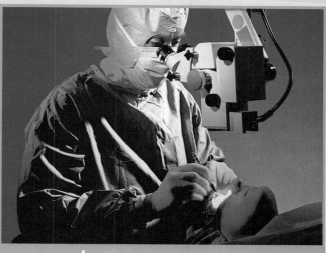

LASER EYE SURGERY

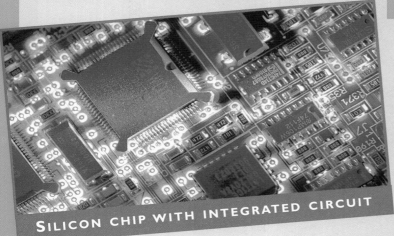

SILICON CHIP WITH INTEGRATED CIRCUIT

b 🔊 📖 KEYWORDS

Look at the keywords in the box. In pairs, try to think of an important advance in each area in the 20th century. Tell the class.

medicine computer technology
entertainment transport energy
communication

Example: We think the discovery of penicillin was really important in medicine.

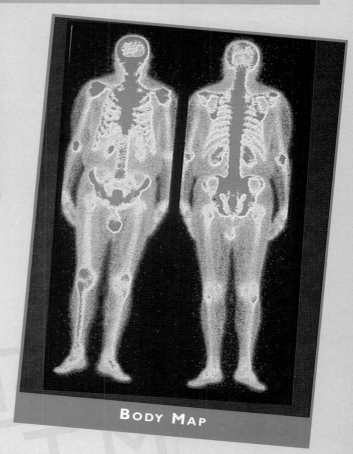

BODY MAP

19 Inventions and Discoveries

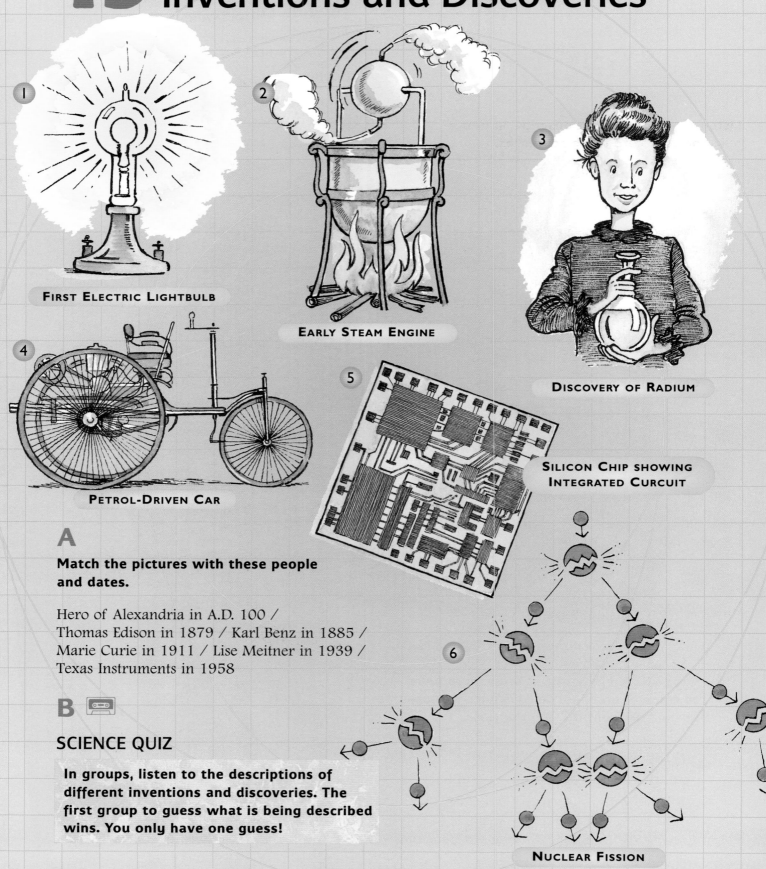

1 FIRST ELECTRIC LIGHTBULB

2 EARLY STEAM ENGINE

3 DISCOVERY OF RADIUM

4 PETROL-DRIVEN CAR

5 SILICON CHIP SHOWING INTEGRATED CURCUIT

6 NUCLEAR FISSION

A

Match the pictures with these people and dates.

Hero of Alexandria in A.D. 100 /
Thomas Edison in 1879 / Karl Benz in 1885 /
Marie Curie in 1911 / Lise Meitner in 1939 /
Texas Instruments in 1958

B 📼

SCIENCE QUIZ

In groups, listen to the descriptions of different inventions and discoveries. The first group to guess what is being described wins. You only have one guess!

Language Focus: Passives

C

Listen again to the first description in the quiz and complete these sentences.

1 This instrument ... the most important in the history of communication.
2 The first long-distance connection ... between New York and Boston in 1884.
3 Before satellites, connections ... by cables.
4 It ... by Alexander Graham Bell in 1876.
5 The first exchange, with operators connecting callers, ... in Connecticut in 1887.
6 These instruments ... in homes and public places, and mobile ones were developed in the 1990s.

D

Find verbs in exercise C which are:

- singular
- plural
- present passive
- past passive

Notice we only include *by* ... when this information is important or not obvious.

E

Write sentences using these cues.

Example: The telephone was invented by Alexander Bell in 1876.

1 the telephone/invent
2 the electric light bulb/invent
3 a steam engine/design
4 silicon chips/produce
5 radium/discover
6 a petrol-driven car/build
7 the first article on nuclear fission/publish

F

In pairs, test your partner on the history of science. Student A looks at number 1 on page 93. Student B looks at number 1 on page 94.

G

INVENTIONS GAME

In pairs, make a list of inventions from the last 50 years for these areas:

music and entertainment
the home
school and work

Examples: electric guitar / microwave oven / fax machine

With another pair, take turns to say inventions from your lists. The pair with the longest list wins.

H

Look up these words in the mini-dictionary and say them aloud. Underline the stressed syllable in each word.

Example: 1 <u>chem</u>istry <u>chem</u>ist <u>chem</u>ical

1	chemistry	chemist	chemical
2	biology	biologist	biological
3	physics	physicist	physical
4	science	scientist	scientific
5	produce	producer	product
6	reserve	reservation	

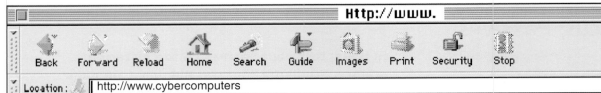

Http://www.

| Back | Forward | Reload | Home | Search | Guide | Images | Print | Security | Stop |

Location: http://www.cybercomputers

Do you know how a telephone works? Or a television? Probably not. It's the same with computers. They are used for writing, reading, storing and transferring information by people in all kinds of jobs, but not many people know how they work.

There are three basic parts of a computer: the **input unit**, **CPU** (central processing unit) and the **output unit**.

Imagine you want to store and send some information. First of all, you put the information into the CPU using the **keyboard** and a **mouse**. If you already have the information on a **floppy disk** or **compact disc**, you can put this in directly.

When the information reaches the CPU, it is read using the **ROM** (read-only memory), and then it is stored in the **RAM** (random-access memory). Confusing? Not really – think of the ROM as the eyes and brain, and the RAM as the memory.

Finally, the information is sent to the **output unit**. This means you can look at it on the **VDU** (visual display unit), which is like a television, tell the **printer** to print a copy on paper, or send it to another computer using a **modem**.

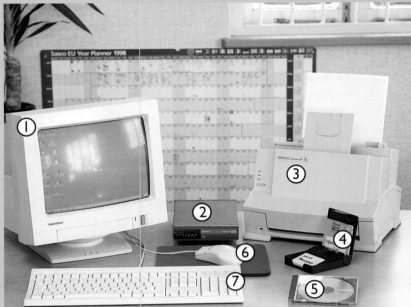

Modems let you send information along telephone lines to other computers anywhere in the world. With a modem you can connect your computer to millions of other computers via the **Internet** and use the **World Wide Web** (WWW). The Web uses **hypertext** – like the words in blue on this page. If you 'click' your mouse on these words, you get more details or links to other pages – a bit like a whole library at your fingertips!

A KEYWORDS

Match the objects in the photograph with these words.

laser printer   box of floppy disks
VDU   compact disc (CD)   keyboard
modem   mouse

B

Read the description of how a computer works. Then copy and complete the diagram.

| **Input** Keyboard, ^{1} . . ., ^{2} . . . or compact disc | → | **CPU** ROM ^{3} . . . | → | **Output** Printer, ^{4} . . ., or ^{5} . . . |

C

Read the text again. Find the words and expressions which link the different stages of the process.

Example: First of all, ...

D

Match the objects with what they do.

1	a printer	**a**	is a kind of television you use for displaying data
2	a VDU	**b**	is a thing that is used for sending data along phone lines
3	a mouse	**c**	is something you use for printing data
4	a keyboard	**d**	is a kind of typewriter that is used for typing data
5	a modem	**e**	is something you use for 'clicking' on words and symbols

E

Write sentences like the ones in exercise D about these objects.

microwave oven / fridge / light bulb / satellite / telephone / pocket calculator / laser / telescope / photocopier / computer / floppy disk

Example: A microwave oven is a thing that is used for heating food quickly.

F

GUESSING GAME

In groups, take turns to think of an object. The others try to guess what it is, asking only ten questions.

Example: A: Is it large?
B: No.
C: Do you use it for travelling?
B: No.
D: Do you use it for cleaning things?
B: No.

G

Look at the pictures. Describe the process of making silicon chips linking the stages and using the passive.

Example: First of all, silicon is made into crystals from sand.

1 Silicon/make into crystals from sand

2 Crystal/shape into long rods
3 Rods/cut into thin slices

4 Circuit/design on computer
5 Designs/transfer onto silicon slices by photographic process
6 Circuits/treat with chemicals

7 Slices/cut up into individual chips

21 Women in Science

A

In pairs, how many famous scientists can you name in two minutes? Tell the class.

B

Read the text and match these titles with the paragraphs.

Inequality Today / The Discovery of DNA / Famous Names / Recent Research

C

What do the underlined words refer to? Paragraph numbers are in brackets.

Example: it (1) = the list

it (1) / they (1) / they (2) / it (2) / it (3) / they (4)

WOMEN SCIENTISTS

1 Can you name five famous scientists? You probably can: Einstein, Newton, Leonardo da Vinci, Galileo, Edison ... The list goes on. But how many women scientists can you name? Marie Curie and, er, ... the list seems to stop before <u>it</u> starts. Why is this? Is it because there haven't been any prominent women scientists yet? Is it because women aren't as clever as men? Or is it because <u>they</u> aren't interested in science? The answer is a big 'no'.

2 In the past, of course, women weren't allowed to go to university! <u>They</u> designed and invented many things but often men took the credit. For instance, Rosalind Franklin had already taken an X-ray photo of the structure of DNA by 1952. <u>It</u> was shown to two male scientists, Watson and Crick, without her permission. In 1962, they were given the Nobel Prize for their discovery of DNA!

3 More recently, women scientists have begun to get the recognition they deserve. For example: Dr Martha Piper has done significant research into the development of premature babies. She has already developed a program which may help eliminate physical disabilities in babies.

Dr Marianne English is a meteorologist and has designed programs to predict the weather. Although scientists can't control the weather yet, it may already be possible to make rain fall in areas of the world which desperately need <u>it</u>.

4 Unfortunately discrimination still remains. Women researchers aren't allocated as much money for their projects and <u>they</u> aren't paid as much as men yet either.

Language Focus:
Still, yet and *already*

D

Match the word in italics in each sentence with the explanation of its use.

> 1 She has *already* developed a program . . .
> 2 Although scientists can't control the weather *yet* . . .
> 3 Unfortunately discrimination *still* remains.
>
> a used when something hasn't happened, will happen in the future
> b used when something has happened sooner than expected
> c used when a situation hasn't changed

E

Find other examples of *still, yet* and *already* in the text and match them with a, b or c above.

F

Read the text and complete it with *still, yet* or *already*.

Scientists have ¹ ... developed computers that can think but they ² ... haven't invented a computer that is as complex as the human brain. Lynn Sutherland is a young computer scientist. Her main interest is artificial or computer intelligence, but she has ³ ... worked in many areas, including sport. She has tried to design a program to predict the results of football matches – of course, she hasn't succeeded ⁴ ...!

G

Write sentences using *still, yet* and *already* and the cues below.

Example: A: They have already designed digital watches.

1 they / design / digital watches
2 astronauts / land / on another planet
3 aeroplanes / travel / faster than sound
4 meteorologists / find a way of controlling the weather
5 scientists / discover / particles smaller than an atom
6 space rockets / travel at the speed of light
7 astronomers / discover life on another planet
8 engineers / build magnetic trains

H

NAME THE SCIENTIST

> **In pairs, prepare some questions about scientists. Then test another pair.**
>
> *Examples:* Name the scientist who invented the telephone.
> Name a scientist from the USA.
> Name a woman scientist.

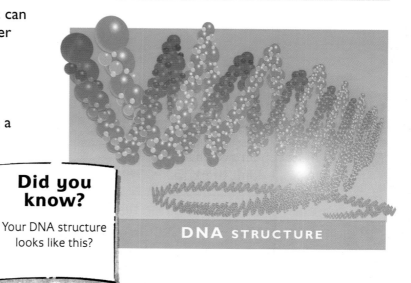

DNA STRUCTURE

Did you know?

Your DNA structure looks like this?

A HEALTHY FUTURE

Jan Bloor takes a look at modern medicine

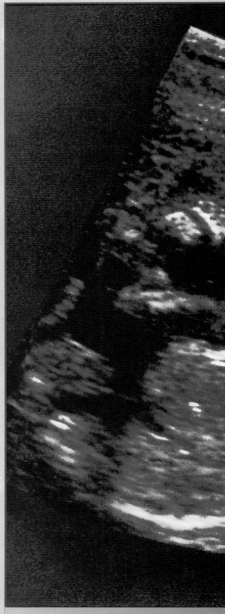

ULTRASOUND

1 Two hundred years ago, visiting the doctor was often a painful experience. For many illnesses, doctors used to 'bleed' their patients. Leeches were used – small animals which suck the blood. Doctors thought that illness was caused by 'bad' blood. Before the discovery of penicillin in 1928, you could die if a cut became infected.

2 Nowadays, medicine is a fast-moving area of science. To make a diagnosis. a doctor can do many tests, perhaps with the help of modern technology such as computers and lasers.

- **NMR** (nuclear magnetic resonance) scan. Powerful magnets scan the patient's body and build up a picture on a computer screen.
- **CAT** (computerised axial tomography) scan. A computer takes X-ray photos of the body from many different angles, and then builds up a three-dimensional picture – much better than a normal X-ray.
- **Ultrasound** Sound waves are passed through a part of the body and a computer image is constructed. This is a very safe test and is often used to look at unborn babies.

3 After a diagnosis, treatment is prescribed. It could be a simple antibiotic or something more complex.

- **Lasers** Lasers are used to cut parts of the body or to destroy dangerous cells. They can clear heart blockages or do delicate operations on eyes.
- **Microsurgery** Doctors use powerful microscopes to perform operations on very small parts of the body.

4 Who knows what the future holds? Perhaps a cure for cancer or AIDS or maybe even the common cold is just around the corner.

A  KEYWORDS

Look at the words in the box. In pairs, take turns to ask questions.

Example: A: Have you ever had 'flu?
B: No, I don't think so.

> 'flu   a broken arm or leg   a blood test
> an operation   a tooth taken out   an X-ray
> a sprained ankle   an eye test   a sore throat

B

Read the text and match these titles with the paragraphs.

The Painful Past
The Future
Tests
Modern Surgery

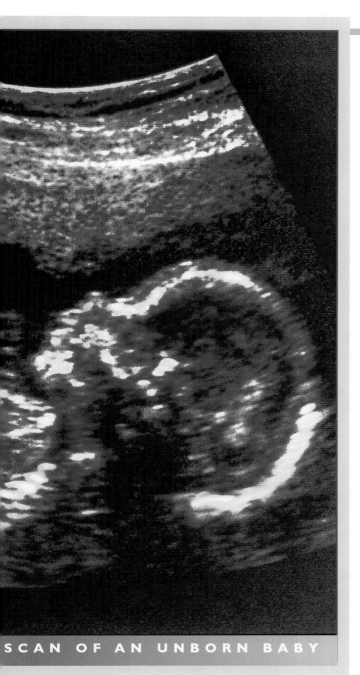

SCAN OF AN UNBORN BABY

D KEYWORDS

Copy and complete the table then listen to three conversations with a doctor.

SYMPTOMS	DIAGNOSIS	TREATMENT
sore throat, [1]..., [2]... and temperature	'flu	stay in bed, take [3]... and drink lots of [4]...
pain in [5]...	sprained ankle	[6]... and a tight bandage
pain in [7]..., been [8]... 3 times	appendicitis	go to hospital for an [9]...

E KEYWORDS

Listen to the first conversation in exercise D again and complete these sentences.

Doctor	Patient
[1] . . . the matter?	[2] . . . a terrible sore throat.
[3] . . . me have a look at your throat	My muscles [4] . . .
I'm [5] . . . you've got 'flu. You'll [7] . . . stay in bed	I [6]... really weak.

C

Read the text again and answer these questions.

1 Why did doctors use leeches?
2 Why was the discovery of penicillin so important?
3 Which technique uses sound waves?
4 Why is a CAT scan better than a normal X-ray?
5 Why is ultrasound especially suitable for looking at unborn babies?

F

In pairs, take turns to be the doctor and a patient. The patient explains some symptoms to the doctor. The doctor makes a diagnosis and recommends treatment.

Did you know?

Leeches have been used again in modern medicine! After some operations they are used to help blood circulation.

23 Fluency

A

Listen to the TV programme about a new invention. Copy and complete the table.

Invention	a clockwork [1] ...
Reason	no radios in poor areas
Advantages	cheap – no [2] ... or batteries
How it works	• wind it up with a [3] ... • electricity is generated • [4] ... is stored and released
Interest	South Africa, the [5] ... and UNICEF

Final Writing Task: Inventions

Science project

B

In pairs, write a report about an invention. It can be a real one or you can invent your own.

Stage 1: Planning Draw a table like the one in exercise A and write notes about the invention.

Stage 2: Writing Use your notes to write three paragraphs:

• the reason for the invention/where the idea came from
• how it works
• advantages/who will use it

Remember to include:
• linking words - *first of all, when, and then, finally*
• some passive sentences

Stage 3: Checking Check your report for punctuation, spelling, linking words and passives. Don't forget to include illustrations.

Stage 4: Feedback Give your report to your partner to read. Your partner grades it like this:

1 difficult to understand, confusing
2 quite clear
3 very clear and easy to understand

Display your reports on the wall or in a class folder.

Final Speaking Task: A Survey

C

Ask other students the questions in this survey. You can add a question of your own if you want. Make a note of the answers.

THE SCIENCE SURVEY

1 Do you enjoy science lessons?
   a) usually b) sometimes c) rarely

2 Which is your favourite science subject?
   a) physics b) chemistry c) biology

3 Are you good at mathematics?
   a) yes b) average c) no

4 Would you like to do more science experiments in school?
   a) yes b) no

5 Have you ever bought a science book or magazine?
   a) yes b) no

6 Do you use a computer?
   a) a lot b) sometimes c) rarely

D LEARN TO LEARN

Look at the diagrams and say which of these things they are used for.

- writing down ideas
- classifying vocabulary
- showing information
- explaining how things work

Now draw a bar graph to show the results of the survey you did in exercise C.

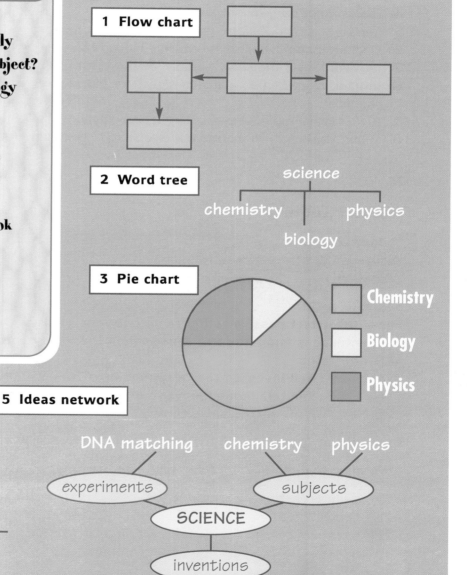

1 Flow chart

2 Word tree

science
chemistry   physics
biology

3 Pie chart

Chemistry
Biology
Physics

4 Bar graph

good at maths
like science
5 10 15 20 25 30
NUMBER OF STUDENTS

5 Ideas network

DNA matching   chemistry   physics
experiments   subjects
SCIENCE
inventions
computer   telephone

24 Consolidation

Grammar

A

Use the cues to make passive sentences in the present or past tense.

Example: 1 Data is stored in the computer's memory.

1 Data / store / in the computer's memory
2 Atoms / split / to produce heat and electricity
3 A plan for a helicopter / make / by Leonardo da Vinci
4 Lasers / not use / in surgery in the 1960s
5 Messages / send / along phone lines using a modem
6 Doctors thought illnesses / cause / by bad blood
7 In NMR tests / the body / scan / by powerful magnets
8 In nuclear medicine / patients / give / a radioactive chemical
9 A clockwork radio / invent / by Trevor Baylis
10 When you wind up the radio / electricity / generate

B

PASSIVE GAME

Make two teams.
Team A says a sentence in the active.
Team B changes the sentence into the passive.

Score, like this:
For each correct passive sentence you get one point.
If a sentence is impossible to change then the other team gets one point.
***Example:* A: Bell invented the telephone in 1876.**
B: The telephone is invented for Bell in 1876.
T: Wrong! One point to A.

Bonus point for team A if you can say the correct answer.

Stop after five minutes and see who has the most points.

C

Complete the sentences with *still, yet* or *already*.

ATOMIC FACTS

You probably [1] ... know that everything is made up of small particles called atoms. But did you know these atomic facts?

- scientists have discovered particles smaller than atoms called quarks, but they haven't proved they exist [2] ... .

- on the Sun, hydrogen atoms fuse to release energy as heat. Scientists [3] ... haven't found a way of creating fusion on Earth.

- medical scientists have [4] ... found ways of killing certain cancer cells. However, they haven't found a cure for all cancers [5] ... .

- exposure to gamma rays can keep food fresh longer – but many people [6] ... aren't happy with the idea – they are afraid of the harmful effects of radiation.

- the first nuclear reactor was built in 1942. But there have [7] ... been many major accidents such as Windscale (UK), Three-Mile Island (USA) and Chernobyl (Ukraine).

Vocabulary

D 🔑 KEYWORDS

Complete the sentences with these verbs.

> look at print out wind up think of build up

1 How many scientists can you ... ?
2 You have to ... the radio like a clock.
3 Ultrasound is often used to ... unborn babies.
4 CAT scans ... a three-dimensional X-ray picture.
5 You can ... data on paper.

E 🔑 KEYWORDS

Copy and complete the table.

AREA	JOB	ADJECTIVE
science	...	...
...	biologist	...
...	chemist	...
...	...	astronomical

Pronunciation

F ▭

Look at these word stress patterns.

Pattern 1	Pattern 2	Pattern 3
■ ▫ ▫	▫ ■ ▫	▫ ■ ▫ ▫
instrument	direction	biology

Copy the table. Then listen and classify these words according to their stress patterns.

technology / telephone / reaction / invention / atomic / astrology / electric / instruction / photograph / geology / computer / periscope

Now practise saying the words with a partner.

Test Yourself

A (10 points)

Complete the gaps with _still_, _yet_ or _already_.

1 Scientists have ... started to map DNA.
2 We've ... discovered cures for some cancers.
3 There is ... a lot of research to do into cancer.
4 The project began in 1990 and scientists haven't finished ... .
5 We've ... travelled faster than the speed of sound, but we can't go at the speed of light ... .
6 They are ... experimenting, but they haven't got any results ... .
7 Doctors ... prescribe simple but effective drugs like aspirins every day.
8 It is amazing that they have progressed so much ... .

B (5 points)

Write each sentence using the words given so that it means the same as the first one.

1 Einstein proposed the Theory of Relativity. The Theory of Relativity . . .

2 They don't use leeches often nowadays. Leeches . . .

3 They gave Watson and Crick the Nobel Prize. Watson and Crick . . .

4 Karl Benz invented the petrol-driven car. The petrol-driven car . . .

5 They make silicon crystals from sand. Silicon crystals . . .

Extra Time

Look at Reading Club 4 on page 99.

Module Check

Language Check

PASSIVE
Present simple
Sound waves **are passed** through the body.
A computer image **is built** up.

Past simple
Leeches **were used** to bleed patients.
They thought illness **was caused** by bad blood.

STILL / YET / ALREADY
Scientists have **already** succeeded in killing some types of cancer cells but they haven't discovered a cure **yet.** They are **still** trying.

Keyword Check

- **Make sure you know the meaning of these words and expressions.**
- **Put important new words in your vocabulary book.**

Subjects: physics, chemistry, biology, medicine, communication, the environment
Computers: keyboard, mouse, VDU, floppy disk, compact disc, printer, modem, the Internet
Medicine: symptoms, diagnosis, treatment, patient, operation, sore throat, headache, temperature
Verbs: design, invent, discover, think of, print out, build up, wind up
Abbreviations: WWW, CPU, CD-ROM
Wordbuilding: science / scientist / scientific, biology / biologist / biological
Explaining uses: a thing that is used for ... + ing, a thing you use for ... + ing, a kind of ...
Describing pain and illness: I feel really ..., I've got a terrible ..., I've got a pain in my ..., I feel really ..., My ... aches/hurts

- **Try to add more words to each list.**

Module diary

- **Which was your favourite lesson in module 4? Why?**
  Example: Lesson 19, because I enjoyed the quiz.
- **Write down something interesting or unusual from this module.**
  Example: They sometimes use leeches after operations!
- **What was your score in the *Test Yourself* activity?**
- **Give yourself a mark for these structures:**
  - Passives
  - Articles
  A I understand them.
  B I sometimes make mistakes.
  C I don't understand them.
- **Look through the texts in this module. Which was the most difficult?**

Completing a diagram (Lesson 20)
Matching titles and paragraphs (21 and 22)
Finding references to words (21)
Finding answers to specific questions (22)

- **When you are speaking English in class, which of these do you do?**
  A If I don't know a word, I start the sentence again in a different way.
  B I use words like: *well, you know* . . . to give me time to think if I don't remember a word.
  C I don't worry too much about grammar; I just try to communicate.
- **How many new words have you written in your vocabulary book?**

CRIME

Module Objectives
In this module you will ...

Read about some crazy crimes, an extract from a crime novel and statements to the police

Talk
Listen about different crimes and try to solve a murder mystery to a murder story, police interviews and life story of Ned Kelly

Practise using the past perfect tense and modal verbs for speculation

Your **final tasks** will be to **write** a crime narrative and play a judging game.

Lead-in

a KEYWORDS

Match the keywords with the newspaper headlines.

Example: a = bank robbery

murder burglary shoplifting mugging
drug smuggling bank robbery

b

In pairs, decide which are the most and least serious crimes. Tell the class.

Example: We think murder is the most serious.
It depends ...

Gang get away with $2.000.000 a

Thief takes family savings- AND their pet hamster! b

Boy (10) stole sweets from shop on way to school c

Young girl found DEAD in park d

Customs police find marijuana in ice-cream lorry e

GRANNY ROBBED IN STREET f

25 Crazy Crimes

P.C. George Wilkins

said: 'I saw Mr James Sprinkle driving a milk float dangerously down Cambourne Hill. Several drivers had to pull over. At first I could not keep up with him. But when the milk float got to the bottom of the hill, I jumped off my bicycle, and tried to arrest him. He shouted: "I will not stop. I am mad for speed!" But soon after that, he crashed into the back of Mr Arthur Jenkin's car.'

During her interview, Ms Sabina Firm said: 'It is my fault. I told Henry I would leave him if he did not get me a colour television. So he went out and came back with one. At that moment, the police came in and arrested Henry for shoplifting. One of the detectives said they caught him quickly because he has his name, Henry Smith, tattooed on his forehead. He had taken a taxi and told the driver: "You have seen nothing – OK? You have not seen Henry Smith."'

MRS ANGELA ARBUTHNOT was charged at Dover court with two serious offences: trying to smuggle animals into Britain, and hitting a customs officer. Mr Reginald Hobhouse, the customs officer, told the court: 'When I was looking through Mrs Arbuthnot's suitcase, I saw two pet hamsters. When I tried to pick one of them up, it bit me and Mrs Arbuthnot shouted: "You mustn't touch Ronny, he's very sensitive." Then, she hit me over the head with her handbag.'

A

Read the newspaper reports. Use the mini-dictionary to check any difficult words. Then match the reports with these crimes.

- shoplifting
- smuggling
- dangerous driving

One of the stories is false. Which one do you think it is?

B

Read the reports again. Is this information true, false or not mentioned?

1 It is illegal to drive a milk float at more than thirty miles an hour.
2 Mr Sprinkle crashed the milk float.
3 The police arrested Sabina for shoplifting.
4 It was difficult for the detectives to catch Henry Smith.
5 You can't take animals into Britain.
6 Mrs Arbuthnot bit the customs officer.

C KEYWORDS

Complete the sentences with verbs from the box in the correct form.

> pull over keep up with look through come back

1 She ran very fast and I couldn't ... her.
2 At the airport the customs officer took my bag and ... it.
3 He went out to buy some bread but he didn't ... .
4 He was driving dangerously, so the policeman asked him to ... .

D

Do the sentences describe laws or what a person recommends/tells you to do?

1 It is *illegal* to drive a milk float at more than 30 mph.
2 You *mustn't* tell anybody you have seen me.
3 You *can't* take animals into Britain.
4 You *mustn't* touch Ronny.

E

Which of the things below are illegal (I) for people under sixteen in your country and which are not recommendable (NR)?

Example: drive a car ~ (I)

- drive a car
- forget your homework
- work full-time
- work part-time
- buy cigarettes
- leave home
- get married
- vote in an election
- go to a casino
- eat chewing gum in class
- go to a discotheque

F

Using the ideas in exercise E, write six sentences.

Example: You mustn't forget your homework.

G

Read about four crimes and decide what they are. Then in pairs discuss which crime is the most and which is the least serious.

1 Susan has five small children and very little money. She stole food from a supermarket.
2 Samantha is a professional thief. She stole a lot of silver from a rich family's house.
3 Eric needed a lot of money for a medical operation for his mother. He held up a bank to get it.
4 Mr Smith brought his pet dog into Britain illegally.

Did you know?

In Waterloo, Nebraska, it is illegal for a barber to eat onions between the hours of 7 a.m. and 7 p.m.

26 Detectives

A

In pairs, think of famous detectives from films, television and books. Tell the class.

Example: Brad Pitt was a detective in the film *Seven*. We like Sherlock Holmes stories.

B

Look at the photo of the detective Cordelia Gray. Why is she not a typical fictional detective?

C

Read the text and answer these questions. You can use the mini-dictionary.

1   Where is Cordelia in the photo?
2   Was Mark normally a clean and tidy person?
3   What things had Mark left untidy or dirty before he died? Why, do you think?
4   What other things were strange?
5   Who do you think had washed the second mug?
6   What did Cordelia begin to suspect?

S he had examined the cottage in accordance with the Super's instructions. What did she now know about the dead boy? What had she seen? What could she deduce?

He had been almost obsessively neat and tidy. His garden tools were wiped after use and carefully put away, his kitchen had been painted and was clean and ordered. Yet he had abandoned his digging less than two feet from the end of a row; had left the uncleaned fork in the earth; had dropped his gardening shoes casually at the back door. He had apparently burnt all his papers before

Language Focus: Past perfect

D

Copy and complete the table with these headings:

auxiliary   participle   subject

...	...	...	
she	had	examined	the cottage

Now add more sentences from the text to your table.

killing himself, yet he had left his coffee mug unwashed. He had made himself a stew for his supper which he hadn't touched.

. . . But suppose someone had visited him that evening.

. . . But suppose it wasn't Mark who had wished to conceal the fact that a visitor had called that night; suppose it wasn't Mark who had washed and put away the second mug; suppose it was the visitor who had wished to conceal the fact of his presence.

. . . A word dancing at the back of Cordelia's mind, . . . came suddenly into focus and, for the first time, spelt out clearly the blood-stained word.

M U R D E R.

(from An Unsuitable Job for a Woman by P.D. James)

E

Look at the diagram and answer the question below.

past		present	future
He had stopped digging before the end of the row. *(past perfect)*	MARK'S DEATH	Cordelia looking for clues	WILL SHE SOLVE THE MURDER?

In which situation do we use the past perfect, a, b or c?

a to describe an activity at a specific time in the past
b to describe an action in the past
c to emphasise that one action in the past happened before something else in the past

F

Look at the picture of Cordelia Gray's room. Write five sentences about what you think the detective had done before she left the room.

Example: She had burnt some papers.

G

In groups, compare your sentences and work out a theory about what she had done before she left the room.

Example: First she had . . .
Then she had . . .
Next she had . . .
After that, she had . . .

One person from each group reports the theory to the rest of the class.

H

LONGMAN DICTIONARY SKILLS

Use the mini-dictionary to make a new word from the word in brackets and complete the sentences.

1 He was convicted of ... an old woman in the street. (*mug*)
2 After the ..., they locked all the doors securely at night. (*rob*)
3 The ... got away through the bathroom window. (*burgle*)
4 We saw a very ... film on TV last night. (*fun*)
5 He never wins. He is always ... . (*success*)
6 When she won the money, she spent it ... . (*extravagant*)

27 Murder in Marbella

On the night of August 11th Jimmy Capaldi was murdered in his mansion in Marbella. His friends and family were staying with him at the time.

Jimmy Capaldi

Susan Capaldi

Brigite Muller

Madame Lebrun

Jimmy Capaldi Jr

Arthur Williams

Stephanie Capaldi

Christos Popodopolis

Jaime Peñafiel

Lady Julia Hamilton

Bruce Maxwell

A 🔊 🔑 KEYWORDS

Read the beginning of the story. Listen and find out the nationality of the people and their relationship with Jimmy Capaldi.

> business partner butler doctor daughter
> wife son biographer cook secretary
> daughter's boyfriend

Language Focus: Speculation and deduction

B

Listen and complete these sentences.

couldn't / must / may / could / might / can't

1 Susan Capaldi ... be the murderer. She was his wife.
2 Stephanie Capaldi loved her father. She ... be the one who did it.
3 Brigite Muller ... have killed him, but why? She was only his secretary.
4 Williams ... know who the killer is. Butlers always know what is happening.
5 Bruce Maxwell ... have shot him. But what motive did he have?
6 I think Jimmy Capaldi Jr. ... have done it because he wanted his father's money.

C

Match the modal verbs with the descriptions.

1	must	**a**	weak possibility
2	may	**b**	impossibility
3	could/might	**c**	certainty
4	can't/couldn't	**d**	possibility

Which sentences in exercise B speculate about the present and which about the past?

D

Rewrite these sentences with the correct form of the verb.

Example: Lady Julia Hamilton couldn't have killed Capaldi.

1 Lady Julia Hamilton couldn't *kill/have killed* Capaldi.
2 Now Susan Capaldi must *feel/have felt* sad.
3 Dr Popodopolis could *murder/have murdered* Capaldi.
4 Madame Lebrun may *know/have known* who the killer is.
5 Jaime Peñafiel might *shoot/have shot* Capaldi.

E

Look at the information on page 95. Write five sentences speculating about the murderer and why he/she did it.

Example: It could be Stephanie. She could have killed her father because she wanted to marry Jaime, and her father tried to stop her.

F

In groups agree on a theory about the murder. Report it to the class.

28 Alibis

A

Look at the plan of Jimmy Capaldi's mansion. Can you remember where he was murdered?

B

Listen to Inspector Garcia checking the statements of four of the people. Match their names with the places on the plan.

Example: 1 Susan Capaldi – A (drawing room)

C

Read these statements. Now listen again and find out what is wrong with them.

Example: Susan Capaldi wasn't reading a book, she was writing a letter.

Susan Capaldi: Statement   1

I was in the drawing room reading a book. I could hear the butler next door opening bottles until about 9.15. Then at about 9.25 I heard someone in the hall. Then at 9.30 I heard the shot.

S. Capaldi

Dr Christos Popodopolis: Statement   2

I was fishing at the pond. At about 9.25 I saw a woman in the library. Then I heard the shot.

C. Popodopolis

Brigite Muller: Statement

I was watching a tennis match on TV. I didn't hear anything.

B. Muller

Bruce Maxwell: Statement   4

I was cleaning my car. It is a lovely old Rolls and I never let anyone else touch it. At 9.15 I saw a tall person in the library with Mr Capaldi.

B. Maxwell.

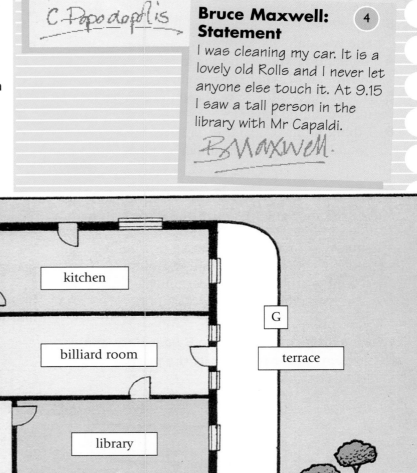

D

Listen to Inspector Garcia checking information and complete the questions with question tags.

Example: 1 = weren't you?

1 You were in the drawing room reading a book, ... ?
2 You could hear the butler opening bottles until about 9.15, ... ?
3 At 9.25 you heard someone in the hall, ... ?
4 You were fishing at the pond, ... ?
5 It was a woman, ... ?
6 You didn't hear anything, ... ?
7 You weren't watching TV, ... ?

E

PRONUNCIATION

Listen again. Which of the question tags:

a check a statement you think is true?
b check information you think is suspicious or incorrect?

Listen and repeat the question tags.

F

In pairs, check the other suspects' statements. They may not be true! Student A looks at number 2 on page 93. Student B looks at number 2 on page 94. Write notes to help you find the murderer.

Example: 9.20 front door open / 9.25 somebody in hall / 9.30 shot

G

Write down who the murderer is on a piece of paper. Put your name on it and give it to your teacher.

H

Now listen to the confession of the murderer. Were you right? What was the real motive for the murder?

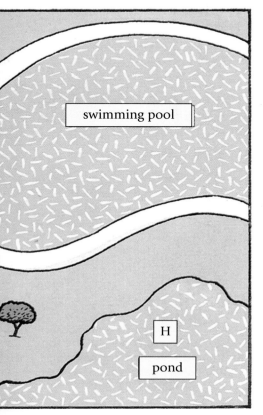

swimming pool

H

pond

Did you know?

Interpol is an international organisation which hunts criminals all over the world. The headquarters is in a quiet suburb of Paris.

B

Listen to the story again and correct the information in these sentences.

1 Ned's father was an Englishman.
2 The police said Dan Kelly had stolen a car.
3 The Kelly gang hid in the desert.
4 Ned Kelly wore armour made from wood.
5 A police officer shot Ned in the arm.

Do you think it was fair that they hanged him?

C LEARN TO LEARN

In pairs, discuss your answers to these questions.

1 What do you do when you know that you have made a mistake?
   a I stop speaking.
   b I continue speaking normally.
   c I try to correct it.

2 What do you do when your partner makes a very simple mistake?
   a I do nothing.   **b** I correct it.
   c I laugh at him/her.

3 Should your teacher correct all your mistakes when you are speaking?
   a Yes, all of them.   **b** Only important ones.
   c No, because I get nervous.

A

Listen to the story of the Australian outlaw Ned Kelly and complete the timeline.

1855	¹ . . .
1870	In trouble with ² . . .
1878	Ned shot and injured ³ . . .
	Formed gang with ⁴ . . .
1879	⁵ . . . men joined the gang.
1880 (June)	Captured town of Glenrowan. Police killed ⁶ . . . members of gang. Injured Ned in ⁷ . . .
1880 (End)	Hanged in Melbourne. Last words: 'Such is ⁸ . . .'

Did you know?

A burglar tried to get into a supermarket through a window but it was too small. He took off his clothes and threw them through the window, but still couldn't get through. He had to ask a policeman for help!

Final Speaking Task: Judging Game

D

In groups, play a judging game.

- Write these words on small pieces of paper and put them on the desk face down.

mugging

shoplifting

murder

burglary

drug smuggling

bank robbery

- Take turns to pick up one of the pieces of paper. Imagine you had committed that crime. Prepare your ideas.
- Tell your story to the group.

Example: I was at the airport. A nice old woman asked me to take one of her bags through customs because it was heavy. The customs police looked through the bag and found some dangerous drugs. I told them it wasn't my bag, but they didn't believe me!

- As judges, the others ask you questions and decide what the punishment should be.

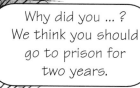

Why did you ... ? We think you should go to prison for two years.

Final Writing Task: A Crime Story

E

Write a short story about a crime that went wrong. It can be amusing or serious.

Stage 1: Planning Make notes for paragraphs about these things:

- *Background:* what was the crime? / who did it and why? / what had they done to prepare for it?
- *Situation:* what happened / was happening at the start?
- *What happened:* how did it go wrong? / what was the punishment?

Stage 2: Writing Use your notes to write three paragraphs. Remember to include linking words: first, then, next, after that, when, while, suddenly, in the end.

Stage 3: Checking Check your story for punctuation, spelling, linking words and past tenses.

Stage 4: Feedback Give your story to your partner to read and evaluate for presentation and interest. Use the table below to give marks:

Presentation	Interest
1 nearly impossible to read	1 boring
2 difficult to read	2 not very interesting
3 reasonable handwriting	3 quite interesting
4 clear and tidy	4 interesting
5 very clearly written and very tidy	5 a very exciting story

30 Consolidation

Grammar

A

VERB TENNIS GAME

> **In pairs, take turns to think of a verb and then make sentences using these tenses in this order:**
>
> past perfect / past simple / past continuous
>
> *Example:* A: (do) I **had done** my homework.
> B: We **did** the shopping.
> A: They **were doing** a project.
> B: (go) She **had gone** to the bank.

B

Make sentences using the past simple and past perfect.

Example: **1** I **ran** to school because I **had got up** late.

1 I / run to school /because / I / get up late
2 When I / arrive / the children / go to bed
3 They / be hungry / because / they / not eat
4 I / phone Mike / because / he / leave a message
5 We / be tired / because / we / not sleep
6 I / not recognise Maria / because / I / not see her for years

C

Complete the sentences with *must, might, can't* or *could*.

Example: 1 He must be rich.

1 He's got a castle in France. He ... be rich.
2 The murderer ... have had a motive.
3 She was near the library, so she ... have killed him.
4 He was near the window, so he ... have seen something.
5 She wasn't there, so she ... have done it.

D

How did the burglar get into the house? Look at the drawing of the house for clues. Then write five sentences about your theory.

Example: He could have climbed over the wall.

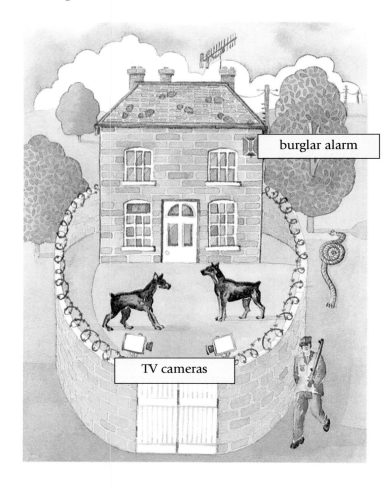

burglar alarm

TV cameras

E

In pairs, speculate about the following situations.

Example: 1 She might be sad. Or she could be peeling onions!

1 A girl is crying.
2 Your friend didn't answer the phone.
3 There was water on the living room floor.
4 The front door of your house is open.

Vocabulary

F  KEYWORDS

Complete the following text by replacing the verbs in brackets with these verbs.

get away / get to / come back / put on /
break in / look through

The burglar (arrived at) ¹ ... the house and
(entered violently) ² ... through the back window.
He was (checking) ³ ... the cupboards when the
owner (returned) ⁴ ... . The burglar (placed on his
face) ⁵ ... a mask, but couldn't (escape) ⁶ ... because
the police were waiting for him in the garden!

G  KEYWORDS

Match these words.

1	steal	**a**	a bank
2	rob	**b**	a house
3	mug	**c**	a cassette player
4	burgle	**d**	in a supermarket
5	shoplift	**e**	a person

Pronunciation

H

**Copy the table below. Listen to these two
vowel sounds. Then listen to five more
sentences and put the verbs into the correct
group according to the sound.**

Group 1 / æ /	Group 2 / ʌ /
drank	drunk

**Listen again and repeat the sentences. Look
through your vocabulary book and find five
more words with each sound.**

Test Yourself

A (10 points)

**Complete the story below with the verbs in
the past simple or past perfect.**

Lord Macaulay was on holiday in Rome. One
evening, after he ¹ ... (have) an excellent meal, he
² ... (go out) to look around. Suddenly, a man ³ ...
(knock) against him. Soon afterwards, Macaulay
⁴ ... (notice) that his watch was missing, and he
thought the man ⁵ ... (steal) it. Macaulay ⁶ ... (run)
after the man. He shouted at him in English and ⁷
... (take) his watch. The man didn't understand.
Macaulay then returned to his hotel. When he ⁸ ...
(get back) to his hotel, the receptionist said:
'Excuse me, signor. I ⁹ ... (find) your watch in the
dining room after you ¹⁰ ... (go out).'

B (5 points)

Complete the text with these words:

might have / can't have / must have (x2) /
couldn't have

Macaulay ¹ ... taken off his watch while he was
having dinner. He ² ... remembered doing this.
The other man ³ ... been a doctor in a hurry to
visit a patient. He ⁴ ... spoken English because he
didn't understand Macaulay. He ⁵ ... felt terrible
when the receptionist gave him his watch.

C (5 points)

Complete the definitions with one word.

1 A ... robs someone in the street violently.
2 A ... deliberately kills someone.
3 A ... steals small things from shops.
4 A ... breaks into houses to steal things.
5 A ... brings things into a country secretly.

Extra Time

Look at Reading Club 5 on page 100.

Module Check

Language Check

PAST PERFECT
He **had dropped** his gardening shoes.
He **hadn't touched** his supper.
Had somebody **murdered** him?

SPECULATION AND DEDUCTION

About the present
They **must** be telling the truth.
She **can't/couldn't** be the murderer.
He **may/might** know who the murderer is.

About the past
She **can't/couldn't** have done it.
Peñafiel **may/might** have killed him.
Maxwell **could** have shot him.
The butler **must** have done it.

Keyword Check

- **Make sure** you know the meaning of these words and expressions.
- **Put important** new words in your vocabulary book.

Crimes and criminals: murder/murderer, mugging/mugger, shoplifting/shoplifter
Nationalities and jobs: Australian businessman, Greek doctor, French cook, German secretary, British butler
Places: cottage, mansion, dining room, kitchen, library, drawing room
Verbs: keep up with, come back, look through, get away, break into
Expressing prohibition: You can't drive until you're eigthteen. You mustn't do that! It is illegal to smoke in public buildings.
Checking information: You were in the kitchen, weren't you? You live near here, don't you?
Giving opinions: We think the butler did it. In our opinion, he should go to prison.

- **Try to add more words to each list.**

Module diary

- **Which was your favourite lesson in module 5? Why?**
- **Write down something interesting or unusual from this module.**
  Example: The story of Ned Kelly.
- **Look back and find an exercise that was difficult for you.**
  Example: Lesson 26 – the reading exercises.
- **What was your score in the *Test Yourself* activity?**

- **Give yourself a mark for these structures:**
  - Past perfect
  - Speculation and deduction
  A I understand it.
  B I sometimes make mistakes.
  C I don't understand it .
- **Look through your vocabulary book and list five very important words that you have learnt in this module.**

CINEMA

Lead-in

Module Objectives In this module you will …

Read magazine articles, film reviews; an interview and a video cover

Talk about films and practise asking for and giving permission

Listen to a film programme, a scene from a home-made film and the story of a film

Practise using the third conditional, reported orders, requests and statements, indefinite pronouns.

Your **final tasks** will be to **write** a film review and to **perform** a short film scene.

1

Air Force One

2

Men in Black

3

a  KEYWORDS

What kind of films are in these photos?

comedy crime romantic science fiction
horror war historical western
thriller disaster action adventure

b  KEYWORDS

Look at the expressions in the box. In pairs, talk about your favourite films.

Example: A: I like *Jurassic Park*. It's a good science fiction film.
B: Why?
A: Well, it's got spectacular special effects and …

good acting (not) worth seeing
an excellent performance by . . .
good photography an exciting story
spectacular special effects

79

31 Film Directors

STEVEN
A CELE

He is, quite simply, the most successful film director ever to walk the planet. 5 Join us for a tour through the imagination of Steven Spielberg.

Spielberg's first 10 major box-office success was *Jaws*, a superb film about a killer shark. It demonstrated Spielberg's ability to pla with his audiences in the same way as Hitchcock 15 *Jaws* was a brilliant technical success despite many difficulties while filming, including mechanical problems with Bruce, the artificial shark.

After this, there were a few disastrous flops like the comedy *1941*. If he had continued to make unpopu 20 films, his name would have disappeared from the film

---

A

In pairs, list and talk about the Spielberg films you have seen.

Example: I saw *Raiders of the Lost Ark*, it was brilliant.

B

Read the article about Spielberg. Find examples of the kinds of film below.

Example: 1 = *Jaws*

> 1 a box-office success   2 a blockbuster
> 3 a flop   4 a sequel   5 an Oscar winner

C

Now answer these questions.

1 What other film director is Spielberg similar to?
2 What caused problems while filming *Jaws*?
3 Who gave Spielberg the idea for the *Indiana Jones* films?
4 Where did the inspiration for *E.T.* come from?
5 What was *Schindler's List* about?
6 Who does *Jurassic Park* appeal to?

Language Focus: Conditional (3)

D

Copy and complete the table with these words.

have / past perfect / past participle

CONDITION	CONSEQUENCE
if + ...	would + ... + ...

In which situation do we use the third conditional, a, b or c?

a to talk about future possibility
b to talk about things that didn't happen in the past
c to talk about imaginary situations in the present

SPIELBERG:
R A T I O N

world. But he also made more fantastic box-office successes like *Raiders Of The Lost Ark* and *Close Encounters Of The Third Kind*. Spielberg's friend George Lucas gave him the idea for the *Indiana Jones* films in
5 Hawaii. If they hadn't been on the beach together making a sandcastle, perhaps Lucas would not have thought about recreating the adventures he loved as a boy. Spielberg's own childhood was the foundation for the brilliant modern fairytale *E.T.*

0 Despite massive popular success, Spielberg failed to win an Oscar with more serious films like *The Color Purple*. Then with *Schindler's List*, a three hour movie about the Holocaust, he won Best Director Award. In the same year he made the dinosaur
35 blockbuster *Jurassic Park*. With its sequel *The Lost World* and the slave drama *Amistad*, Spielberg again tries to show that he can appeal to both young and adult audiences. This may be difficult, but if anyone can do it, Steven Spielberg is that man.

E

Put the verbs in brackets into the correct tense and complete the sentences.

Example: 1 If Spielberg hadn't made a lot of blockbusters, he wouldn't have become the most successful film director ever.

1 If Spielberg …. (not make) a lot of blockbusters, he …. (not become) the most successful film director ever.
2 If Jimmy Capaldi …. (give) his butler some money, Williams …. (not kill) him.
3 If she …. (use) some protection cream, she …. (not burn) her skin.
4 If Ned Kelly …. (not injure) a policeman, he …. (not become) an outlaw.

5 If you …. (be) to Barbados, you …. (have) a relaxing holiday.
6 If he …. (have) enough money, he …. (buy) videos of all the Indiana Jones films.

F

Copy and complete the table for indefinite pronouns.

PERSON		THING
anybody	anyone	anything
somebody	………………	………………
nobody	no one	………………
everybody	………………	………………

G

Complete these sentences with indefinite pronouns.

Example: 1 = nobody

1 … liked that film. It was a disastrous flop.
2 I know … who goes to the cinema four times a week. He's a film fanatic.
3 There is … interesting in that film.
It's terrible!
4 … in my family watches sci-fi films. We all think they're great.
5 I think George Clooney is fantastic. There's … special about him.
6 I don't know … about the cinema. I never remember titles or names of actors.

a

c

b

2 This romantic comedy involves two single parents (Michelle Pfeiffer and George Clooney) who agree to look after each other's kids. *One Fine Day* is about boring real-world problems which aren't really very funny. Despite this, the romance and chemistry between Pfeiffer and Clooney is magical, as they chase each other around a rainy New York. Pfeiffer is wonderful and Clooney is gorgeous. This film has lots of charm and sex appeal. Don't miss it!

1 This sequel to *Jurassic Park*, one of the biggest box-office successes ever, is disappointing. The special effects of Spielberg's *The Lost World* are brilliant and the dinosaurs look even more real than before. However, this $76 million blockbuster offers very little else. The acting, apart from a solid performance by Jeff Goldblum (Dr Ian Malcom), is uninspiring. The dialogue is weak and the story is unconvincing, especially the ending. The film lasts 134 minutes and, if you aren't a dinosaur fanatic, it isn't really worth seeing.

3 *Con Air* is about a plane that transports convicts around the USA. On this trip is, "goodie", Cameron Poe (Nicholas Cage). After eight years in prison, Poe is going home. The plane is captured by the criminals and the action starts. It is pursued by a US Marshall (John Cusack) and the climax comes when the plane lands in Las Vegas. This excellent film is exciting and sophisticated at the same time, with some brilliant individual performances and plenty of explosions and action. It is definitely worth seeing!

A

Are you a film-lover? In pairs, ask and answer these questions.

1 How often do you go to the cinema?
2 What kinds of films do you watch?
3 How often do you watch films on video?
4 How often do you watch films on TV?
5 Who is your favourite actor / actress / director?
6 Do you ever read magazines about films?

B

Look at the film reviews and match them with the pictures. Which review is negative?

C

Read the reviews again and answer these questions.

1 What is the best thing about *The Lost World*?
2 Who is the best actor in it?
3 What is *One Fine Day* about?
4 What is the best thing about the film?
5 What is *Con Air* about?
6 What are the two best things about the film?

D KEYWORDS

Are these adjectives positive or negative? Use the mini-dictionary.

> magical disappointing excellent brilliant wonderful exciting uninspiring weak unconvincing funny sophisticated

Example: magical +

E

Choose a film you have seen recently. Copy and complete the table.

FILM PROFILE

TITLE:	Batman and Robin
STORY:	Mr Freeze steals all the diamonds in Gotham city – Batman and Robin try to stop him
DIRECTOR:	Joel Schumacher
CAST:	Arnold Schwarzenegger / George Clooney / Chris O' Donnell / Uma Thurman / Alicia Silverstone
RATING:	4/10 unconvincing
ACTING:	Schwarzenegger 9/10 Clooney 7/10 Thurman 8/10
STORY:	3/10 terrible
SPECIAL EFFECTS:	4/10 weak
RECOMMENDATION:	Not worth seeing.

F

In pairs, talk about the film.

Example: A: What's it called?
B: It's called *Batman and Robin*.
A: What's it about?
B: Well, Mr Freeze . . .
A: Who's in it?

Who said that?

'If I made *Cinderella* the audience would immediately be looking for a dead body in the coach.' (Alfred Hitchcock)

33 Making Films

A 🔑 KEYWORDS

Which of these jobs would you like to do?

> sound technician lighting technician director
> set manager camera crew actress actor
> producer scriptwriter director of photography

B 📖

**Read the text about making the Addams Family.
Are these sentences true or false?**

1 The film was a failure because of the problems.
2 A lot of people had health problems during filming.
3 Uncle Fester cut his ear off.
4 Paramount Pictures had a lot of financial problems.
5 The producer knew it was going to be a good film.

The Addams Family

The production of the highly successful film *The Addams Family* was marked by a series of crises. First, the script for the film had to be rewritten again and again. Originally done by scriptwriters Carol Thompson and Larry Wilson, the final version was written by the novelist Paul Rudnick.

Then the twenty weeks of filming were full of minor disasters. After three weeks the director, Barry Sonnenfield, actually passed out on set and filming had to be suspended until he recovered. Not long after that, the director of photography, Owen Roizman, walked out to go to another movie. Then his replacement, Gayl Tattersoll, was rushed off to hospital for several days. Next came the actors, with leading actor Raúl Julia (Gomez) off with eye problems and Christopher Lloyd (Uncle Fester) nearly losing his ear in a fight scene!

Worse than all this, however, were the financial problems for producer Scott Rudin. Three-quarters of the way through the film the backers of the movie, Orion Pictures, decided to sell the film to Paramount Pictures because of desperate money problems.

Sonnenfield and Rudin had a tough time but they managed to concentrate on the shooting of the film. 'I always try to remember two things,' said the sensible Rudin on set. 'One, how good the movie is. And two … that it's almost over!'

C KEYWORDS

Which of the jobs in exercise A are mentioned in the text?

Language Focus: Reported requests/orders

D

Copy the table and put these words at the top of the correct column.

ask/tell   subject   action   object

...	...	...	...
1 The director	asked	the set manager	to change the colour of the table
2 The producer	told	the actress	to repeat the scene
3 The producer	asked	the director	not to spend a lot of money.

E

Read these questions, then listen to a scene from a film and answer them.

1 Who does Joanna ask permission from to go to London?
   a the head teacher   **b** her class teacher   **c** her English teacher
2 Why does Mr Edwards not give his permission at first?
   a It would be dangerous.   **b** Joanna has exams.
   c There is no money.
3 Why does Mr Edwards give his permission in the end?
   a He is pleased with her work.   **b** He thinks acting is a good job.   **c** She promises to study more.

F

Listen again and match the parts of the sentences.

1 The director told the set manager   **a** to come in and sit down.
2 The director told John   **b** to move the table a little.
3 The head teacher asked Joanna   **c** to let her take the day off school.
4 Joanna asked the head teacher   **d** to do extra work after school.
5 The head teacher told Joanna   **e** to be really serious.

G

PRONUNCIATION

Listen to six sentences from the film scene. How do the speakers sound?

polite / sleepy / worried / angry / happy / relaxed / nervous / polite

H KEYWORDS

Look at the expressions below. Which are formal and which informal?

Permission 1
A: Is it all right if I go out tonight?
B: OK, you can.
A: Can I go to the cinema tomorrow night?
B: No, you can't.

Permission 2
A: Would it be all right if I took the day off school?
B: Yes, that's all right. / No, I'm afraid you can't.

I DICTIONARY SKILLS

Find compound words and phrases in the mini-dictionary and write questions like these.

What do we call:
1 a machine that *washes dishes*?
2 a *calculator* that you can carry in your *pocket*?
3 a *bag* that you can *sleep* in?
4 somebody whose *weight* is *over* what it should be?

34 Where Are They Now?

Macaulay Culkin

Christina Ricci

Shirley Temple

Charlie Korsmo

Tatum O'Neal

A

In pairs, talk about films you have seen with child stars. Write down the names of the children. Compare your list with other pairs.

Example: There was a young girl in *The Adams Family* - we think she was Christina Ricci.

B 🖭

Which one of the child stars in the photos is still acting? Listen to the film programme and find out.

C 🖭

Listen again. True or false?

1 Jodie Foster and Elizabeth Taylor were famous child stars.
2 Shirley Temple was a big box-office success in Hollywood in the 1930s.
3 Tatum O'Neal won an Oscar in 1970.
4 Macaulay Culkin made over $10 million for *Home Alone 2*.
5 Charlie Korsmo gave up acting when he was thirteen.
6 Christina Ricci starred in *Casper* when she was eighteen.

Language Focus: Reported statements

D

Look at the reported statements in the box. Write the actual words that the writer said in the interview.

Example: 'She's just written a book about child stars in Hollywood.'

1 The presenter said that Janet Caesar had just written a book about child stars in Hollywood.
2 The writer said that some of the famous child stars became famous actors and actresses.
3 She said that there are very few child stars that become adult stars.
4 She said Shirley Temple had given up acting and later had become an ambassador!
5 She said Christina Ricci was still acting and was successful as a teenager.
6 She said there would be a lot more child stars in the future.

(Notice that when we report people saying things which are still true, we sometimes don't change the verb tense.)

E

Copy and complete the table.

DIRECT SPEECH	REPORTED SPEECH
present simple	present simple or ....
present continuous	past continuous
past simple	....
present perfect	....
will	would

Find examples of these tense changes in exercise D.

F

Imagine you have interviewed Sue White. Write a report of the interview.

Example: Her name is Sue White and she told me ...

'My name's Sue White and I work with baby animals in films. Of course, if a dog or a cat is the star of a film, it has a professional trainer, but sometimes the script includes puppies and kittens. Then it's my job to look after them. Usually that means looking after about four or five little animals. I'm glad I didn't work with the film *101 Dalmatians*! I've worked mainly in Hollywood but at the moment I'm working on a film in England. Next week we're going to start filming. I think it will be great fun!'

G

FILM QUIZ

In pairs, student A turns to number 3 on page 93 and student B turns to number 3 on page 94. Find out how much your partner knows about the cinema! Use this type of question.

Example: A: Name the famous actress who appeared in *Batman and Robin*.
B: Sharon Stone?
A: No. Uma Thurman.

When you finish, make up more questions for your partner to answer.

Fluency

A

Which of these things should you do when watching films in English?

a *before* watching **b** *while* watching **c** *after* watching

1 Read a review of it in the newspaper or on the video cover.
2 Evaluate how difficult it was and why (how fast characters spoke, accents, etc.).
3 Follow the film by using the pictures – you only need to understand a little of the dialogue.
4 Use the pause and rewind buttons, if you are watching it on video.

Classic Videos:
Emerald Forest

This is one of director John Boorman's most interesting films and it is based on a true story. The film is set in the Indonesian forest and is about the destruction of the rain forests. An Australian engineer called Bill is working on a dam and shows his family around. His young son Tommy gets lost and disappears. He is kidnapped by a tribe of Indians called 'The Invisible People'. Bill continues every year to look for his son in the forest, but without success. After five years of looking he finds Tommy, now a teenage boy living with the Indians. He dresses like them and cannot speak English. He asks his father for help against the dam which is going to destroy their lands. In the final scene, there is a terrible explosion and the dam is destroyed. Tommy goes back to live with his family and they are all very happy. This film is quite slow and boring in parts. However, some of the acting is not very good. Although there is good photography of the rain forest, the end to the story is very exciting. It is definitely worth seeing!

B

Read the film review from a school magazine. Which of these things is wrong with it?

1 There are no clear paragraphs.
2 There are a lot of grammatical mistakes.
3 It gives too much information about the story.
4 There are a lot of spelling mistakes.
5 The conclusions are contradictory.

C

Read this explanation.

However: Negative sentence followed by *However*, + positive sentence.
Example: The story of *Terminator* is weak. However, the special effects are great.

Although: *Although* + negative part of sentence, + positive part of sentence.
Example: *Although* the dialogue is unconvincing, the acting is excellent.

Now re-write the underlined sentences of the video review correctly.

D

There are five factual mistakes in the story of *The Emerald Forest*. Listen and correct them.

Example: 1 = the film is set in the Amazon forest

E LEARN TO LEARN

Grade the listening activity.

☆☆☆ very difficult   ☆☆ OK   ☆ easy

Final Writing Task:
A Film Review

Film project

F

Write a review of a film you have seen recently.

Stage 1: Planning Look at Lesson 32 again. Read the film reviews and the profile you wrote for exercise E. Add more information.

Stage 2: Writing Use the table to write the review. Be careful with your conclusions. Use *however* or *although* to compare good and bad points about the film.

Stage 3: Checking Check your review for mistakes. Then write a final version. If possible, add photos from magazines.

Stage 4: Feedback Give your review to your partner to read. If he/she has seen the film find out if he/she agrees with it.

Final Speaking Task:
Act A Scene

G

Act out a short scene from a film you have seen.

• In groups, write down some notes:

> kind of film (romance / comedy / suspense)
> characters in film (e.g. mother / father /
> daughter) the scene (the situation at the
> beginning / what happens / the ending)

• Everybody helps to write the script (the dialogue).
• Decide who is going to be the director and which roles the actors take. Do some 'rehearsals' for the film.
• Perform it in front of the class and, if possible, video it. When you are watching, grade other performances like this:

1 unconvincing acting and weak story
2 some good acting although the story isn't very good
3 quite good acting and quite interesting story
4 good acting and interesting story
5 excellent acting and very interesting story

Grammar

A

Read this interview with Winona Ryder. Change the underlined sentences into reported speech.

Example: Winona said that her parents had named her after the town of Winona … She said that …

Interviewer:	You have an unusual name. Why are you called Winona?
Winona:	<u>My parents named me after the town of Winona in Minnesota where I was born. My parents were hippies, so when I was young, we moved to a commune in California.</u>
Interviewer:	When did you make your first film?
Winona:	<u>I made my first film, *Lucas*, in 1986. After that I played teenage roles in several films.</u>
Interviewer:	You were in a Coppola film, weren't you?
Winona:	Yes, <u>when I met Coppola, he offered me a starring role in *Dracula*.</u>
Interviewer:	Have you ever won an Oscar?
Winona:	No, but <u>*Age of Innocence*, which was nominated for an Oscar, made me famous.</u>
Interviewer:	What other films have you made?
Winona:	Well, <u>I've made lots of other films, including *Looking for Richard* and *Alien Resurrection*, both with Sigourney Weaver.</u>

B

Complete the sentences below.

1 If her parents …. (not live) in Winona, her name …. (not be) Winona.
2 If she …. (not love) acting, she …. (not study) at the American Conservatory Theater.
3 If she …. (not meet) Francis Ford Coppola, she …. (not play) a star role in Dracula.
4 If *Age of Innocence* …. (not be) so successful internationally, she …. (not become) so famous.

C

MINI-DICTIONARY GAME

Look through the mini-dictionary and find two words you don't know. Write a definition of each word. Then invent two other definitions.

Example: a flop – something that is not successful (correct definition)
– a person who is very boring (false definition)
– a café where people use the Internet (false definition)

In groups, read out your definitions. The others must guess which is the correct one.

D

Combine the words in the table to write ten sentences about TV programmes you watch.

Example: Gladiators is very exciting. *The Saint* is absolutely brilliant!

not very (−) quite (+) very (++)	funny / interesting exciting/good
really/absolutely (+++)	excellent / wonderful / brilliant / great / magical
quite (−) very (− −)	unconvincing / weak disappointing / boring
really/absolutely (− − −)	terrible / awful

Vocabulary

E

Match the words below.

Example: 1 = c

1 science	**4** romantic	**a** star	**d** office
2 special	**5** child	**b** comedy	**e** writer
3 box	**6** script	**c** fiction	**f** effects

F

Complete the sentences with these verbs.

give up / go on / look after / look for

1 After that performance, she ... to win an Oscar in her next film.
2 He ... acting after he had a lot of personal problems.
3 I ... information about Sigourney Weaver last night on the Internet.
4 She ... her brother when he was a baby.

Pronunciation

G 📼

Listen to the words and names below and repeat them, being careful to pronounce the initial 's' correctly.

start / spectacular / slow / Spielberg / strange / sport / star / special / scriptwriter / Scottish / story / Schwarzenegger / study / stop

Who said that?

When Humphrey Bogart was introduced to Rock Hudson at a party, he said, 'Rock - huh?'
'Yes, sir,' Hudson replied.
'Well,' said Bogart, 'You look pretty soft to me, Rock.'

Test Yourself

A (5 points)

Change into reported speech.

1 I told my friend, Bob, 'George Clooney is starring this week in *Batman and Robin*.'
2 Bob said, 'I've seen *Batman and Robin*.'
3 I said, 'I want to see the film too.'
4 My mother said, 'Finish your homework first!'
5 I asked Bob, 'Will you lend the money to see the film?'

B (10 points)

Complete these third conditional sentences.

1 If I .... (have) enough money, I .... (buy) those jeans.
2 She .... (do) better in the writing task if she .... (bring) her dictionary to class.
3 The film .... (be) more exciting if the actors .... (be) better.
4 If he .... (speak) English all the time in class, he .... (pass) that exam.
5 The actor .... (walk) out if the director .... (tell) him to do it again.

C (5 points)

Use the scale to grade the adjectives below.

bad (−) very bad (− −) very, very bad (− − −)
very good (++) very, very good (+++)

1 absolutely terrible   4 very exciting
2 really brilliant   5 awful
3 disappointing

Extra Time

Look at Reading Club 6 on page 101.

Module Check

Keyword Check

- **Make sure you know the meaning of these words and expressions.**
- **Put important new words in your vocabulary book.**

Kinds of film: comedy, crime, romantic, science fiction, horror, western, action, thriller

Films: special effects, photography, the set, acting, performance by ..., blockbuster, flop, box-office success

Film people: (child) star, producer, director, scriptwriter, light/sound technician, camera crew

Positive adjectives: brilliant, excellent, spectacular, great, magical, funny, interesting, sophisticated, wonderful, exciting

Negative adjectives: terrible, disappointing, unconvincing, uninspiring, weak, boring

Verbs: give up, look for, look after, go on to

Comparing: The acting is good. *However*, the story is weak. *Although* the acting is good, the story is weak.

Recommending: It's (definitely) worth seeing. It's not worth seeing. Don't miss it!

Asking for permission: Is it all right if I go? Can I go?

Giving/refusing permission: OK, you can. Yes, it's OK. No, you can't. No, I'm afraid you can't.

Language Check

CONDITIONAL TYPE 3
If I **had started** acting when I was young, I **would have been** a good actor.
If he **had not had** family problems, he **would have continued** acting.

REPORTED REQUESTS/ORDERS
She **asked** me **to buy** cinema tickets for Saturday.
He **told** them **to wait** quietly.

REPORTED STATEMENTS
'I **enjoy** horror films.' He said (that) he **enjoys** horror films.
'I **live** in Hollywood.' He said he **lived** in Hollywood.
'**I'm making** a film in Australia.' He said he **was making** a film in Australia.
'I **won** an Oscar last year.' He said he **had won** an Oscar last year.
'I **have won** two Oscars in my life.' He said he **had won** two Oscars in his life,
'I **will make** my next film in South America.' He said he **would make** his next film in South America..

INDEFINITE PRONOUNS
Someone invited me to a party. I didn't know **anybody** there. **Everybody** was from another school. **Nobody** danced with me.
There is **nothing** to do on Sunday afternoons. **Everything** is closed.
Is there **anything** I can do?
There's **something** I wanted to ask you.

Module diary

- **Which were the most interesting films and film stars in this module for you?**
- **Grade the listening texts in this module:**
  ☆☆☆ very difficult ☆☆ OK ☆ easy
  - film scene dialogues (Lesson 33)
  - film programme about child stars (Lesson 34)
  - the story of *The Emerald Forest* (Lesson 35)
- **Assess your performance in the Final Speaking Task:** as an individual as a group
  A excellent – I/we performed brilliantly!
  B good – I/we participated a lot and did well.
  C not very good – I/we didn't make much effort.

- **What was your score in the *Test Yourself* activity?**
- **Give yourself a mark for these structures:**
  - pronouns
  - relative clauses
- **Look through your writing so far. Which areas do you need to improve?**
  punctuation / spelling / paragraph organisation / vocabulary / verb tenses / linking words
- **Do the end-of-year Self Assessment on page 95.**

1 – Lesson 19

Ask your partner these questions. (The correct answers are underlined.)

1 Who was the first flight in an aeroplane made by?
a) Louis Blériot
b) <u>Orville Wright</u>
c) Wilbur Wright
2 When and where was the first computer developed?
a) in 1960 in Japan
b) in 1957 in America
c) <u>in 1948 in Britain</u>
3 Where was the world's first lighthouse built?
a) <u>near Alexandria in Egypt</u>
b) near Athens in Greece
c) on the coast of China
4 When was the first water closet (toilet) designed?
a) in AD 100 by the Romans ·
b) in 1320 by P. Henlein of Germany
c) <u>in 1589 by J. Harington in England</u>

2 – Lesson 28

Role play. Interview these suspects (your partner). Remember they may not be telling the truth.

Example: You went for a swim at 9 o'clock, didn't you?

Jaime Peñafiel: At 9 o'clock I went for a swim. Then I sat on the terrace for a few minutes. I heard someone talking to Capaldi, but I couldn't hear who it was. After that I heard the shot.

Madame Lebrun: I was working in the kitchen. I went to the dining room and saw the butler just before 9.30.

Jimmy Capaldi Jr: I was playing billiards in the billiard room. At about 9.25 I heard my father talking very loudly in the next room. I couldn't hear who it was.

Imagine you are these people. Use the true information below to answer your partner's questions.

Stephanie Capaldi: sitting in summer house painting – saw someone with white hair in library at 9.25

Williams: in dining room opening bottles until 9.30 – heard nothing

Lady Julia: in breakfast room working – heard butler opening bottles – stopped at about 9.15 – then heard someone in the hall

3 – Lesson 34

Choose five questions. Give extra information to help your partner, if you know it.

1 An Australian actor – starred in *Braveheart.* (Mel Gibson)
2 A place in the south of France – famous film festival. (Cannes)
3 An American actor – starred in *Casablanca.* (Humphrey Bogart)
4 A female pop singer – starred in *Evita.* (Madonna)
5 An Hollywood actress – child star and successful adult actress – starred in *Contact.* (Jodie Foster)
6 An American actor – starred in *Batman and Robin* and *One Fine Day.* (George Clooney)
7 A female director from New Zealand – made *The Piano.* (Jane Campion)
8 A British director – made crime and suspense movies like *Psycho* and *The Birds.* (Hitchcock)
9 An actor from Austria – successful in action and sci-fi films like *Terminator.* (Arnold Schwarzenegger)
10 A Hollywood film actress – became Princess of Monaco – died in a car crash. (Grace Kelly)

Pairwork Activities B

1 – Lesson 19

Ask your partner these questions. (The answers are underlined.)

1 When was the first bicycle built?
  a) 1781 b) 1823 c) <u>1839</u>
2 Who were the radioactive elements radium and polonium discovered by?
  a) <u>Marie Curie</u>
  b) Albert Einstein
  c) E. Rutherford
3 When was plastic first made?
  a) <u>1862</u> b) 1909 c) 1931
4 Where and when was the first telescope made?
  a) <u>in Holland in 1608</u>
  b) in Greece in 200 BC
  c) in the USA in 1808

2 – Lesson 28

Imagine you are these people. Use the true information below to answer your partner's questions.

Jaime Peñafiel: at 9.00 had a swim – then sat on terrace – heard voices in the library – Capaldi and someone who was old – heard shot

Madame Lebrun: was working in the kitchen – went to the dining room after 9.25 – there was nobody there

Jimmy Capaldi Jr: was playing billiards in billiard room – at 9.25 heard voices next door – father talking to somebody with a British accent

Interview these suspects (your partner). Remember they may not be telling the truth.

Example: You were sitting in the summer house painting, weren't you?

Stephanie Capaldi: I was sitting in the summer house painting. At about 9.25 I saw somebody in the library with my father. I couldn't see the person.

Williams: I was in the dining room opening bottles, when I heard the shot.

Lady Julia: I was working in the breakfast room. I could hear the butler in the next room opening bottles all evening. I didn't hear anything else.

3 – Lesson 34

Choose five questions. Give extra information to help your partner, if you know it.

1 A Hollywood actress– sex symbol of 50s – died in 1962. (Marilyn Monroe)
2 A child star – very successful in the 1930s. (Shirley Temple)
3 An American actor – starred in the *Indiana Jones* films and many more. (Harrison Ford)
4 An actress – starred in and produced <u>One Fine Day</u>. (Michelle Pfeiffer)
5 An American actor – starred in *Back to the Future* films. (Michael J Fox)
6 A child star – starred in *The Addams Family* – later starred in *Casper*. (Cristina Ricci)
7 A comic American actor – starred in *The Mask* and *Liar, Liar*. (Jim Carrey)
8 A Scottish actor – became famous in *James Bond* films. (Sean Connery)
9 A German city – important film festival every year. (Berlin)
10 A Hollywood actor – became President of the USA. (Ronald Reagan)

Lesson 27 – Exercise E

Information about the characters:

Susan Capaldi
She didn't love her husband, who was very cruel to her.

Jimmy Capaldi Jr
He had lost a lot of money at the casino recently. When he had asked his father for more money, his father had refused.

Stephanie Capaldi
She was desperately in love with Jaime Peñafiel. Her father had told her that afternoon, that if she married Jaime she would never get any money.

Jaime Peñafiel
He had asked Mr Capaldi for permission to marry his daughter. Mr Capaldi had laughed at him and told him to come back when he was a millionaire.

Bruce Maxwell
He had found out that morning that Mr Capaldi had cheated him and that he would lose millions of dollars. He would probably go bankrupt.

Lady Julia Hamilton
She had shown her book to Mr Capaldi that day. Mr Capaldi had refused permission to publish it.

Dr Popodopolis
The old doctor loved Susan Capaldi like a daughter. He had been her family's doctor since she had been a child. He hated Capaldi.

Brigite Muller
Jimmy Capaldi had promised to divorce his wife and marry her. That evening Jimmy had changed his mind.

Madame Lebrun
Jimmy Capaldi hadn't liked lunch and he had sacked Madame Lebrun.

Williams
Williams had stolen money from the Capaldis. Mr Capaldi had just telephoned the police.

Science: Lead-in P51

All the statements are true.

End-of-year Self-Assessment

Grade yourself in the following way:

A I have no problems
B I sometimes have difficulties
C I have a lot of problems with this

Speaking

- ❏ using English in class
- ❏ giving and find out personal information
- ❏ expressing opinions about fashion, films, music and holidays
- ❏ telling stories
- ❏ role-playing real-life situations

Writing

- ❏ a formal letter
- ❏ reports and profiles
- ❏ a film review
- ❏ a story

Grammar

- ❏ basic tenses (present/past/future)
- ❏ auxiliary verbs
- ❏ conditional sentences
- ❏ modal verbs (*must, might,* etc.)
- ❏ passives
- ❏ pronouns
- ❏ prepositions
- ❏ relative clauses
- ❏ quantity expressions
- ❏ past perfect

Listening

- ❏ to other students in class
- ❏ to your teacher
- ❏ to dialogues on the cassette
- ❏ to pop songs

Reading

- ❏ magazine or newspaper articles
- ❏ extracts from fiction or poems
- ❏ information texts (like encyclopedias)
- ❏ tourist brochures
- ❏ letters

Now write an end-of-year report on your English. See if your teacher agrees!

CHANEL

Where is the centre of fashion? Rome? London? New York? For much of the twentieth century, Paris was the home of 'haute couture', leading the world in elegant design. Among the famous fashion houses was Chanel, perhaps most well-known today for its expensive perfumes.

Gabrielle Chanel, who was always known as 'Coco', was born into a family of peasants in France in 1883. Her parents died when she was young and she worked with her sister, making hats. After the First World War, when she was a nurse, she borrowed some money and set up a little dress shop in her home town. The shop was very successful, so Coco moved to Paris and opened a new shop. She designed her own clothes which became extremely popular.

The secret of her success was that her clothes were simple and comfortable but at the same time elegant. She designed suits with straight, collarless jackets and was the first to make the 'little black dress' that women still love today. Chanel revolutionized women's fashion all over the world. Coco's designs were copied and sold internationally, so most women, who could not afford the real Chanel, were able to be fashionable.

Chanel became the leading fashion house of Paris and the world. Coco also produced perfumes, like the famous Chanel No.5, and was soon a millionairess. She retired in 1938 but sixteen years later, after the Second World War, she made a come back. Chanel's clothes, perfumes and jewellery became as popular as before.

A

Read the text and choose the best answer.

Chanel became a great fashion house because:

a   Coco was French.
b   Coco was a good designer.
c   Coco produced perfumes as well as clothes.

B

Find words in the text which mean:

1   a company which produces elegant clothes.
2   people who work on the land.
3   plain, not decorated.
4   without a collar.
5   completely change the way people think or do things.
6   a return to an earlier position of importance.

C

Read the text again and answer these questions.

1   Which city was the centre of fashion for most of the twentieth century?
2   How did Coco begin in the fashion industry?
3   Why did she move to Paris?
4   In what way were her designs revolutionary?
5   What was Chanel famous for, as well as clothes?
6   How old was she when she made her come back?

A

Read the text quickly and answer the questions.

1 In how many countries were people watching the NetAid concert?

2 What world problem is NetAid fighting against?

events

NetAid

Were you watching TV on Saturday 9th October 1999? Or were you logged on to the Internet? Something very special happened that day.

At the same time, 110,000 people were enjoying the NetAid's pop music concerts in New York, London and Geneva and millions of people in 160 countries around the world were enjoying them on TV or via the Internet. World-famous musicians like The Eurythmics, Robbie Williams, George Michael and Jewel performed. Bono of U2, with others, promoted NetAid to the public.

We had already had LiveAid in the past – a pop concert shown internationally on TV to raise money for famine relief in the poorest countries. Now we had something even more ambitious. The aim of NetAid is to make people aware of poverty in the world. It hopes to make people think about the problems of hunger, refugees, debt, the environment and human rights. It

wants to encourage us to be involved, to do something. That is why NetAid used the Internet, why even during the concert it encouraged us to leave our television and go to the Internet. And after the concert, the NetAid website will continue to link people who are fighting poverty all over the world, helping them to share their time, their resources and their good ideas. If people can come together through the Internet and work together to fight poverty, then the world will be a better place.

B

Find words or expressions in the text for:

1 a time when there is not enough food for people to eat.
2 the state of being poor.
3 people who have to leave their country because they are in danger.
4 money owed.
5 the basic right that everyone has to be treated fairly.
6 being a part of something, being active in something.

C

Read the text again and answer these questions.

1 If people could not go to any of the NetAid concerts, how could they watch them?
2 In what two ways was the NetAid concert more ambitious than LiveAid?
3 What does NetAid believe is the greatest problem in the world?
4 How will the NetAid website help people to be involved?
5 Why do you think NetAid started its campaign with a multi-media pop concert?

Lord of the Flies

Lord of the Flies by William Golding is a novel about a group of British schoolboys who are in a plane that crashes on a deserted island in the Pacific.

These pictures are from an American film of the book, which was made in 1990.

A

Read the first extract and look at picture B. Answer the question.

What is Ralph holding? Why?

Extract 1

Ralph smiled and held up the conch for silence.

'Listen everybody. I've got to have time to think things out. I can't decide what to do straight off. If this isn't an island, we might be rescued straight away. So we've got to decide if this is an island. Everybody must stay round here and wait and not go away. Three of us – if we take more we'd get all mixed and lose each other – three of us will go on an expedition and find out. I'll go, and Jack, and, and ...' He looked round the circle of eager faces. There was no lack of boys to choose from.

'And Simon.'

B

Answer the questions.

1 Who is the leader?
2 Why do you think his arm is hurt?
3 What must the boys find out?
4 Why will only three boys go on the expedition?
5 Which boys go on the expedition?

C

Read the second and third extracts and answer the questions.

Are there any people on the island, or is it deserted?

Extract 2

'There's no village smoke, and no boats,' said Ralph wisely.

'Well make sure later; but I think it's uninhabited.'

'We'll get food,' cried Jack. 'Hunt. Catch things ... until they fetch us.'

Extract 3

Ralph spread his arms.

'All ours.'

They laughed and tumbled and shouted on the mountain.

'I'm hungry.'

When Simon mentioned his hunger the others became aware of theirs.

'Come on,' said Ralph. 'We've found out what we wanted to know.'

D

Answer the questions.

1 If nobody lives on the island, how will the boys get food?
2 How do the boys feel when the three explorers return?
3 What is the first thing they are all going to do?
4 Look at picture C. What do you think will happen in the story?

A

Read the passage and complete the flow chart showing the development of silk.

| natural silk from …. | ⟹ | …. from …. | ⟹ | …. from …. |

The Invention of Nylon

Think for a moment about the things you use every day. What are your shirts or blouses made of? What about your sister's stockings or tights? Does your mother wear a fur coat? What are the carpets in your home made of?

In the past, all these articles were made from natural materials: fur from animal hair, wool from sheep, leather from animal skins, cotton from the cotton plant and silk from silkworms. Women loved to wear silk. It was a luxury material and it was expensive because it was produced in countries like China from silkworms which had to be especially cultivated.

In 1935, a chemist called Wallace Carothers was working at the du Pont chemical company in the USA. He was leading a team who were trying to produce a totally synthetic silk. In 1884, a French chemist had already produced an artificial silk from plants, which was called rayon. Carothers wanted to make a silk fibre from chemicals. After a lot of research he succeeded. The substance, which contained long chains of molecules, was first called polyamide 6,6. This could be used for making a fibre like silk.

The first articles that were made out of the new synthetic fibre, now called nylon, were toothbrushes. Later, it was used to produce fabric for clothes, carpets and even parachutes. Nylon was strong, light, hardwearing and cheap to make. But the greatest success was the production of nylon stockings for women. On their first day of sales, 27th October 1938, in New York, five million pairs of 'nylons' were bought by the enthusiastic public!

B

Answer the questions.

1 In the past, clothes used to be made from natural materials. Is this true today?
2 Why was natural silk a luxury material?
3 Which country made the first artificial silk?
4 Why do we say that nylon was the first totally man-made or synthetic fibre?
5 Why was nylon immediately successful?
6 Which article of clothing made of nylon became tremendously popular?

C

Are these pairs of words similar in meaning (S) or opposites (O)?

1	expensive	cheap
2	produce	make
3	stockings	tights
4	natural	synthetic
5	synthetic	artificial
6	article	thing

A

Read the story. Where do you think it comes from?

a a novel   **b** a local newspaper   **c** a book of true stories   **d** a magazine

Hungry Housebreaker

One winter's day, in the town of Brighton in the south of England, a burglar, William Brady, was sentenced to six months in prison.

The burglary had taken place on a Saturday night. Brady was walking along Lansdowne Avenue. He had been out with friends and it was a long walk home. It was raining and he was feeling cold and miserable. He looked at the lights in the big houses and thought to himself, 'Those people must be warm and happy. They don't need to be out walking on a cold wet night.'

Then he saw that one of the big houses was completely dark. He stopped and listened. There were no sounds from the house. He went up the drive and walked round the house. 'No, there's no one here,' he thought. 'They must have gone away for the weekend.'

He broke into the house through the kitchen window at the back. He looked quickly round the kitchen but there was nothing valuable there. He tried the inside door but it was locked. 'I'll have to smash the door,' he said to himself. 'But first, let's see if there's anything to eat. They might have left some food in the fridge.'

The fridge was full of food. First he had a large pork pie, then he ate a ham sandwich, followed by a chicken sandwich. He finished off with an enormous piece of chocolate cake.

After that, he relaxed in his chair and soon dropped off. He was still sleeping happily when the police came to arrest him the next morning.

B

Find words or expressions in the text to replace the underlined words in these sentences.

1 William Brady was a <u>thief</u>.
2 He was <u>given a punishment</u> of six months in prison.
3 He <u>used force to get inside</u> the house.
4 He was hoping to steal things <u>that were worth a lot of money</u>.
5 The door was <u>closed with a key</u>.
6 He <u>fell asleep</u> in the chair.

C

Read the text again and answer these questions.

1 Why was William Brady sent to prison for six months?
2 Had he stolen anything valuable?
3 How did he get into the house?
4 Why didn't he go into every room in the house?
5 What did he do in the kitchen?
6 How long had he been asleep when the police arrived?
7 Why do you think the police came to arrest him?
8 Do you think that Brady was a professional thief who often broke into houses? Why?/Why not?

Clint Rowe

Part 1

Clint Rowe is the top animal wrangler, a wrangler being someone who trains animals for the movies. He trains dogs and has just got back from Alaska, where he has been with Jed, a 15-year-old half-wolf, half-dog who stars in the film *White Fang*.

'We were up on the coast and the rain came and washed away the snow! Eventually, we used potato flakes to simulate the snow.'

However the film crew's problems weren't over.

'Unfortunately,' Rowe remembers with a smile, 'when the flakes got wet they turned into mashed potato, and the animals started eating it!'

Part 2

To train animals takes time and patience.

'In *White Fang* we had to persuade Jed to put his head underwater to catch a fish, which he didn't want to do. Jed doesn't like water, you see. We took it very slowly and eventually he did it. Usually if the dog feels secure, he'll do whatever you want.'

Isn't it cruel to use animals like this? Rowe doesn't think so.

'They enjoy doing tricks.'

But he thinks it is important for directors to stop when the dogs are tired.

'I'm using a special trailer on this trip, so that the dogs have somewhere to relax when they're not working. I've been on jobs with problems about rest periods, but 90 per cent of film crews are fine. The 10 per cent that, aren't, I really believe should be punished.'

A

Look at the photograph and read the text quickly to answer these questions.

1 What is the dog's name? Why is he unusual?
2 What is Clint Rowe's job? Is he cruel to his dogs?

B

Read Part 1 of the text again and answer these questions.

1 When Clint Rowe was interviewed, where had he been with Jed?
2 What did he tell the interviewer about the weather problems there?
3 What had they used to make artificial snow?
4 Why had this not solved their problem?

C

Read the rest of the text and choose the best answer.

1 Clint Rowe told the interviewer that in the film *White Fang*:
   a Jed had refused to put his head under water.
   b Jed had enjoyed putting his head under water.
   c Jed had obeyed Clint's order to put his head under water.

2 He said that Jed would do what the trainer wanted if he felt:
   a patient.
   b tired.
   c secure.

3 If the trainer had been impatient with the dog:
   a Jed would not have obeyed him.
   b Jed would have done what he was told.
   c Jed would have learnt to catch a fish.

4 Clint Rowe said that it was important to have a rest:
   a when the film director was tired.
   b when the dogs were tired.
   c when the dogs had done some tricks.

Mini-dictionary

This mini-dictionary will help you to understand all the words that are either important to remember or necessary to do the activities. Remember that you don't have to understand every word when you read a text. We recommend that you refer to the **Longman Active Study Dictionary** for words not included here. Remember that this mini-dictionary is not a substitute for a complete dictionary.

Abbreviations used in this mini-dictionary:

adj = adjective	*n* = noun	*prep* = preposition
adv = adverb	*no pl* = no plural form	*pron* = pronoun
conj = conjunction	*pl* = plural	*v* = verb

Aa

abandon /əˈbændən/ *v* to leave or give up completely: *The baby was abandoned by its mother. We abandoned our holiday because we had no money.*

ache /eɪk/ *v* to be painful; to hurt: *Her head ached.*

action /ˈækʃən/ *n* something that you do: *His quick action saved her life. A lot of things happen in action films.*

actor /ˈæktə/ *n* a man who acts in plays or films.

actress /ˈæktrɪs/ *n* a woman who acts in plays or films.

advance /ədˈvɑːns/ *n* **1** forward movement: *the advance of the enemy.* **2** improvement or progress: *There have been great advances in medicine in the last 50 years.*

adventure /ədˈventʃə/ *n* an exciting thing that happens to someone: *He wrote a book about his adventures as a soldier.*

aggression /əˈgreʃən/ *n* (no pl) angry or violent behaviour in which you attack someone.

AIDS /eɪdz/ *n* Acquired Immune Deficiency Syndrome; a very serious disease caused by a virus which breaks down the body's natural defences against infection.

album /ˈælbəm/ *n* **1** a book with empty pages where you can put photographs, stamps, etc. **2** a long-playing record (LP).

alibi /ˈælɪbaɪ/ *n* proof that a person was in another place at the time of a crime and so could not have done it: *He didn't have an alibi for the night of the murder.*

although /ɔːlˈðəʊ/ *conj* **1** in spite of the fact that something is true: *Although it was raining we went for a walk.* **2** but: *We only spent £50, although that doesn't include drinks.*

ankle /ˈæŋkəl/ *n* the part of the leg just above the foot, which can bend.

appeal (to) /əˈpiːl/ *v* to please, attract or interest.

apply /əˈplaɪ/ *v* to ask for something: *I want to apply for the job.*

arrest /əˈrest/ *v* to make someone a prisoner because they are believed to have done something wrong.

article /ˈɑːtɪkəl/ *n* **1** a thing: *articles of clothing.* **2** a piece of writing in a newspaper: *an article about ships.* **3** the words *a* or *an* (= indefinite article) or *the* (= definite article).

aspirin /ˈæsprɪn/ *n* a drug that reduces pain and fever.

astronomy /əsˈtrɒnəmə/ *n* the scientific study of the stars and planets.

astronomer /əsˈtrɒnəmi/ *n* someone whose job is to study the stars and planets.

astronomical /æstrəˈnɒmɪkəl/ *adj* **1** connected with the study of the stars. **2** extremely high (costs or prices).

attraction /əˈtrækʃən/ *n* **1** something that attracts people because it is interesting or enjoyable. **2** when one person is attracted to another because they like them very much.

attractive /əˈtræktɪv/ *adj* pleasing, especially to look at.

avoid /əˈvɔɪd/ *v* to keep away from a person, place or thing: *Are you trying to avoid me?*

awful /ˈɔːfəl/ *adj* **1** very bad or frightening: *an awful accident.* **2** not pleasing; not liked: *That's an awful book.*

Bb

backing musician /ˈbækɪŋ mjuːˌzɪʃən/ *n* a musician who supports the main singer or musician.

bandage /ˈbændɪdʒ/ *n* a long piece of cloth used for covering a wound.

bass guitar /beɪs gɪˈtɑː/ *n* a guitar which makes the lowest sound.

beach /biːtʃ/ *n* a shore covered in sand or stones where people go to swim.

belt /belt/ *n* a piece of cloth or leather worn round the middle of the body: *I need a belt to keep up my trousers.*

biographer /baɪˈɒgrəfə/ *n* a person who writes the story of another person's life.

biological /ˌbaɪəˈlɒdʒɪkəl/ *adj* relating to biology.

biologist /baɪˈɒlədʒɪst/ *n* a person who studies biology.

biology /baɪˈɒlədʒi/ *n* the scientific study of living things.

bleed /bliːd/ *v* (bled, bled, bleeding) to lose blood: *The cut on my arm bled for ages.*

blockbuster /ˈblɒkˌbʌstə/ *n* a very successful film or book.

blood /blʌd/ *n* the red liquid that flows round the body.

blood-stained /ˈblʌdsteɪnd/ *adj* showing a mark where blood has fallen on something.

blouse /blaʊz/ *n* a shirt for women or girls.

blues /bluːz/ *n* (pl n) a type of slow, sad music from the Southern US.

book /bʊk/ *v* to arrange to have something that you want to use later: *I've booked tickets for tomorrow night's show.*

bored (with) /bɔːd/ *adj* feeling tired and uninterested: *She was bored with her job.*

boring /ˈbɔːrɪŋ/ *adj* not interesting; dull: *a boring film.*

box office /ˈbɒks ˌɒfɪs/ *n* a place in a cinema or theatre where you can buy tickets.

boyfriend /ˈbɔɪfrend/ *n* a boy or man who is the special friend of a girl or woman: *Can my boyfriend come to the party?*

break in/into /breɪk ɪntʊ, -tə/ *v* (broke, broken, breaking) to get inside a place using force: *Someone broke in through* the window. *Someone broke into the house through a window.*

break up /ˌbreɪk ʌp/ *v* (**broke, broken, breaking**) **1** to finish a relationship with a boyfriend or girlfriend: *John and Sarah broke up last week.* **2** to stop going to school because the holidays are starting: *We break up next week.*

breeze /briːz/ *n* a light wind.

brilliant /ˈbrɪljənt/ *adj* **1** very bright; shining brightly: *a brilliant colour.* **2** very clever: *a brilliant student.* **3** very good: *The film was brilliant.*

build up /ˌbɪld ʌp/ *v* (**built, built, building**) to increase, develop or become gradually larger: *He has built up a good business over the years.*

burglar /ˈbɜːglə/ *n* a person who breaks into buildings to steal things.

burglary /ˈbɜːgləri/ *n* the crime of entering a building by force and stealing things.

burgle /ˈbɜːgəl/ *v* to break into a building and steal from it.

business partner /ˈbɪznɪs ˌpɑːtnə/ *n* one of the owners of a business.

butler /ˈbʌtlə/ *n* the chief male servant of a house.

Cc

camera crew /ˈkæmərə kruː/ *n* a group of people working together with cameras to make a film.

carry on /ˌkæri ɒn/ *v* to continue: *Carry on with your homework. They carried on talking.*

castle /ˈkɑːsəl/ *n* a large strong building made so no one could attack the people inside.

casual /ˈkæʒuəl/ *adj* **1** not planned or arranged: *a casual meeting.* **2** not used for a special time or place: *He was wearing casual clothes, not his school ones.*

casually /ˈkæʒuəli/ *adv* in a casual way: *casually dressed.*

CD /ˌsiː diː/ *n* compact disc which stores recorded music and speech.

CD-Rom /ˌsiː diː ˈrɒm/ *n* (compact disc read only memory) a CD on which large amounts of information can be stored to be used by a computer.

charge /tʃɑːdʒ/ *v* **1** to ask for money for something: *He only charged me £2 for this book.* **2** to say that a person has done something wrong: *He was charged with stealing a car.* **3** to run or hurry: *The little boy charged into the room.*

chat show /ˈtʃæt ʃəʊ/ *n* a television or radio show in which well-known people talk to each other and are asked questions.

chemical /ˈkemɪkəl/ *n* a substance, especially one made by or used in chemistry.

chemical /ˈkemɪkəl/ *adj* made by chemistry.

chemist /ˈkemɪst/ *n* **1** a person who makes and sells medicines. **2** **chemist's** a shop where medicines and some goods for the house can be bought. **3** a person who studies chemistry.

chemistry /ˈkemɪstri/ *n* (no pl) the science which studies substances like gas, metals, liquids, etc., what they are made of and how they behave.

chip /tʃɪp/ *n* **1** a small piece of fried potato. **2** a very small piece of metal or plastic used in computers to store information or make the computer work. Sometimes called a microchip.

classical /ˈklæsɪkəl/ *adj* (used about music) serious and of lasting importance: *I prefer classical to modern music.*

climax /ˈklaɪmæks/ *n* the most exciting or important point of a story or some action, usually happening near the end: *the climax of the film.*

coat /kəʊt/ *v* to put a thin covering of something on the surface: *The table was coated with dust.*

cold /kəʊld/ *n* **1** an illness of the nose and throat: *I've got a cold.* **2** (no pl) cold weather: *I don't like the cold.*

come back /ˌkʌm bæk/ *v* (**came, come, coming**) to return: *Her parents told her to come back home before ten o'clock.*

comedy /ˈkɒmədi/ *n* a funny play, film, etc; something that makes you laugh.

comfort /ˈkʌmfət/ *n* being free from pain, trouble, etc.

comfortable /ˈkʌmftəbəl, kʌmfət-/ *adj* pleasant to wear, sit in or be in: *This a very comfortable chair.*

commune /ˈkɒmjuːn/ *n* a group of people who live and work as a team for the general good.

communication /kəˌmjuːnɪˈkeɪʃən/ *n* **1** (no pl) the act of speaking or writing to someone and being understood by them: *Communication between people who speak different languages is difficult.* **2** **communications** (*pl n*) road, railways, radio, telephones and all other ways of moving or sending information between places.

compact disc /ˌkɒmpækt ˈdɪsk/ (also **CD**) *n* a type of record with very good sound played on a special machine.

completely /kəmˈpliːtli/ *adv* totally: *Have you completely finished your work?*

complex /ˈkɒmpleks/ *adj* **1** difficult to understand, explain or deal with: *This a very complex problem.* **2** consisting of many closely connected parts: *It's a complex system.*

conscious /ˈkɒnʃəs/ *adj* awake and knowing what is happening around you: *He is badly hurt but still conscious.*

convention /kənˈvenʃən/ *n* **1** a meeting of people with a shared purpose: *a business convention.* **2** the accepted way of doing things.

conventional /kənˈvenʃənəl/ *adj* following accepted customs.

convict /ˈkɒnvɪkt/ *n* a person who has been sent to prison for doing something wrong.

convict /kənˈvɪkt/ *v* to decide in a law court that somebody is guilty of a crime: *He was convicted of murder.*

cook /kʊk/ *n* a person who prepares food for eating.

cool /kuːl/ *adj* **1** not warm, but not very cold: *The room was cool after the sun had gone down.* **2** calm: *Don't get excited about the examination; keep cool.* **3** fashionable: *His hairstyle is really cool.*

cosmetics /kɒzˈmetɪks/ *n* (pl n) substances put on the skin, especially on the face, and on the hair to make you look prettier.

cottage /ˈkɒtɪdʒ/ *n* a small house in the country.

cotton /ˈkɒtn/ *n* (no pl) **1** a plant grown in hot countries for the fine white threads that cover its seeds. **2** thread or cloth made from the cotton plant: *a cotton dress.*

country and western /ˌkʌntri ən ˈwestən/ *n* popular music in the style of the southern and western US.

CPU /ˌsiː piː ˈjuː/ *n* (central processing unit) the part of a computer that controls and organises all its activities.

crazy /ˈkreɪzi/ *adj* **1** very strange or not sensible **2** mad **3** be crazy about to like someone or something very much.

crime /kraɪm/ *n* an action that is wrong and can be punished by the law.

crocodile /ˈkrɒkədaɪl/ *n* a large tropical reptile which has a long body and a long mouth with sharp teeth and which lives in lakes and rivers.

crowd /kraʊd/ *n* a large number of people: *There was a crowd of people waiting at the station.*

crowded /ˈkraʊdɪd/ *adj* full of people: *I don't like the market; it is too crowded.*

cruel /ˈkruːəl/ *adj* liking to hurt other people or animals.

cruelty /'kru:əlti/ *n* (no pl) actions that cause pain to a person or animal: *cruelty to animals.*

cruise /kru:z/ *n* a trip on the sea for pleasure.

cure /kjʊə/ *n* a way of making better: *a cure for an illness.*

customs /'kʌstəmz/ *pl n* a department of the government that controls what is brought into a country.

Dd

dark /dɑ:k/ *adj* **1** like night; not light or bright: *It was getting dark, so we hurried home.* **2** of a deep colour, nearer black than white: *She has dark hair. He wore dark glasses.*

deaf /def/ *adj* not able to hear because you have something wrong with your ears.

dealer /'di:lə/ *n* a person whose job is to buy and sell a certain thing: *a dealer in old cars.*

deck chair /'dek tʃeə/ *n* a type of chair that you can fold until it is flat, and that people sit on outside, especially by the sea.

delicacy /'delɪkəsi/ *n* **1** the quality of being delicate: *She admired the delicacy of the lace table-cloth.* **2** something good to eat that is considered rare or expensive: *Caviar is a great delicacy.*

delicate /'delɪkət/ *adj* **1** easily harmed, damaged or broken: *a delicate glass; a delicate child who is often ill.*

delicately /'delɪkətli/ *adv* carefully.

denim /'denɪm/ *n* (no pl) a strong cloth, usually blue in colour, which is used to make jeans.

department store /dɪ'pɑ:tmənt stɔ:/ *n* a type of shop that is divided into several parts, each of which sells a different kind of goods.

deserted /dɪ'zɜ:tɪd/ *adj* empty of people: *a deserted street.*

design /dɪ'zaɪn/ *v* to make a drawing as a plan for something: *to design a building.*

designer /dɪ'zaɪnə/ *n* a person whose job is to think of ideas for making things and then draw them.

despite /dɪ'spaɪt/ *prep* although something is true: *Despite the bad weather, we enjoyed our holiday.*

diagnosis /ˌdaɪəg'nəʊsɪs/ *n* the act of finding out what is wrong and describing it.

dig /dɪg/ *v* (**dug, dug, digging**) to cut downwards into something: *He is digging in his garden.*

dining room /'daɪnɪŋ ru:m, rʊm/ *n* a room with a table where you can eat meals.

director /dɪ'rektə, daɪ-/ *n* **1** a person who controls a business. **2** someone who directs a play or film, deciding how it is performed or filmed.

disability /ˌdɪsə'bɪləti/ *n* not being able to move your body easily because of some illness or wound: *Blindness is a very serious disability.*

disappointing /ˌdɪsə'pɔɪntɪŋ/ *adj* not as good or as nice as you expected: *a disappointing film.*

disaster /dɪ'zɑ:stə/ *n* something very bad, especially something that happens to a large number of people and causes a lot of damage or harm.

discover /dɪs'kʌvə/ *v* to find something or to learn about something for the first time: *Columbus discovered America.*

dish /dɪʃ/ *n* **1** a plate or container for serving food **2** food cooked or served in a particular way: *a pasta dish*

dishwasher /'dɪʃˌwɒʃə/ *n* a machine that washes dirty plates, etc.

DNA /ˌdi: en 'eɪ/ *n* the substance which carries genetic information in a cell.

drawing room /'drɔ:ɪŋ ru:m, rʊm/ *n* a room where people sit or entertain other people.

dress /dres/ *n* **1** a piece of clothing covering the body and legs that is worn by women and girls. **2** (no pl) clothes of a certain type or for a particular purpose: *fancy dress.*

drug /drʌg/ *n* **1** a medicine. **2** something that people take to change the way they feel or behave: *Many drugs are not allowed by law.*

drum /drʌm/ *n* a musical instrument made of a round hollow box with skin stretched tightly over it, which is beaten.

dye /daɪ/ *v* to give a colour to: *She dyed her hair black.*

Ee

earn /ɜ:n/ *v* to get money in return for work you do: *He has earned a lot of money by working in the evenings.*

earring /'ɪərɪŋ/ *n* a piece of jewellery you wear on your ear.

edge /edʒ/ *n* **1** the outside end of something; the part which is furthest from the middle: *the edge of a plate; the water's edge.* **2** the sharp cutting part of a knife or tool.

electric /ɪ'lektrɪk/ *adj* working by electricity: *an electric cooker.*

energy /'enədʒi/ *n* (no pl) **1** the ability to be active and do a lot without feeling tired. **2** the power that makes machines work and gives heat: *Coal provides energy for lighting the factory.*

entertainment /ˌentə'teɪnmənt/ *n* (no pl) activities which amuse or interest people: *For entertainment we watch television.*

environment /ɪn'vaɪərənmənt/ *n* **1** the conditions of the Earth and of the society surrounding you: *Children need a happy home environment.* **2** the world of land, sea and air you live in: *Cutting down too many trees destroys the environment.*

equipment /ɪ'kwɪpmənt/ *n* (no pl) the things which are used for a particular activity: *office equipment.*

excellent /'eksələnt/ *adj* very good: *This is excellent work, Peter.*

exciting /ɪk'saɪtɪŋ/ *adj* able to give someone strong and pleasant feelings: *exciting news.*

exotic /ɪg'zɒtɪk/ *adj* **1** unusual and exciting: *exotic clothes.* **2** from a distant and interesting country: *exotic food.*

expedition /ˌekspə'dɪʃən/ *n* a long, difficult journey, usually to find out something: *an expedition to find the beginning of the River Nile.*

extravagant /ɪk'strævəgənt/ *adj* spending too much money: *She's very extravagant - she spends all her money on clothes.*

extravagantly /ɪk'strævəgəntli/ *adv* spending too much money: *She is extravagantly generous at Christmas.*

extremely /ɪk'stri:mli/ *adv* very: *I am extremely hot.*

Ff

facilities /fə'sɪlɪtiz/ *pl n* things for you to use, especially in a public place: *sports facilities.*

fail /feɪl/ *v* **1** not to succeed: *Their attempt to win had failed. The crops have failed because of lack of rain.* **2** not to pass an examination: *He failed his English test.*

failure /'feɪljə/ *n* someone or something that does not succeed: *The plan was a failure.*

fair /feə/ *adj* **1** light in colour **2** reasonable and acceptable **3** neither particularly good nor bad.

fame /feɪm/ *n* (no pl) the state of being known and admired by a lot of people.

famous /'feɪməs/ *adj* well-known and admired: *This town is famous for its beautiful buildings.*

fan /fæn/ *n* **1** an instrument for moving the air around you to make you cooler. **2** someone who likes a particular person or thing very much: *I'm a fan of his music | a football fan.*

fantastic /fæn'tæstɪk/ *adj* extremely good, bad or enjoyable.

fashion /'fæʃən/ *n* the way of dressing or doing something that is considered best at one time: *Is it the fashion to wear short skirts? Yes, short skirts are in fashion.*

fashionable /'fæʃənəbəl/ *adj* liked by many people at a particular time: *fashionable clothes.*

fax machine /'fæks məʃi:n/ *n* a machine, joined to a telephone, which you use for sending copies of letters or pictures to another place.

fed up /ˌfɛd 'ʌp/ *adj* not happy because you have had too much of something or because you are annoyed with someone: *I'm fed up with staying at home all day.*

fit /fɪt/ *adj* not ill; well and able to be active as a result of doing sport.

five-star /faɪv stɑ:/ *adj* excellent; top quality: *a five-star hotel.*

flared /fleəd/ *adj* (of trousers or a skirt) shaped to get wider towards the bottom.

flop /flɒp/ *n* an event that is very unsuccessful.

floppy disk /ˌflɒpi 'dɪsk/ *n* a piece of plastic that you can put into a computer and on which information can be stored.

flu /flu:/ *n* (influenza) a disease which is like a bad cold, but more serious.

fold /fəʊld/ *v* to turn part of something over another part: *She folded the letter so that it would fit into her bag.*

fond of /'fɒnd əv/ *adj* liking someone or something: *I'm very fond of you (= I like you very much).*

foolishness /'fu:lɪʃnɪs/ *n* silliness; behaviour that is not sensible.

formal /'fɔ:məl/ *adj* according to accepted rules or customs: *a formal letter; formal clothes.*

formality /fɔ:'mæləti/ *n* careful attention to rules and behaviour: *There's no formality in everyday life.*

freezing /'fri:zɪŋ/ *adj* very cold: *I'm freezing! It's freezing outside.*

friendly /'frendli/ *adj* kind and helpful: *He is friendly to us all.*

frightened /'fraɪtənd/ *adj* afraid: *He's frightened of dogs.*

funny /'fʌni/ *adj* **1** making you laugh; amusing: *a funny joke.* **2** strange; unusual: *What's that funny smell?*

fur /fɜ:/ *n* (no pl) the soft hair on some animals: *Cats have fur.*

fuse /fju:z/ *v* to stop working, or to make something stop working, because the wire connection in an electric system has melted.

Gg

gambler /'gæmblə/ *n* someone who tries to win money on horse races, games, cards, etc.

gang /gæŋ/ *n* **1** a group of people working together, e.g. building workers or criminals. **2** a group of young people, usually young men, who cause trouble.

get away /ˌget ə'weɪ/ *v* (**got, got, getting**) to escape, e.g. from the scene of a crime: *The thieves got away with the money.*

get to /get tu:/ *v* **1** to arrive: *What time did you get to London?* **2** to annoy or upset someone

give up /ˌgɪv 'ʌp/ *v* (**gave, gave, given**) to stop having or doing something: *She's trying to give up smoking.*

glamorous /'glæmərəs/ *adj* having glamour.

glamour /'glæmə/ *n* a special quality of charm and beauty; attractiveness: *She added a touch of glamour by wearing a beautiful dress.*

go with /gəʊ wɪð/ *v* to match or suit something in colour or style: *These shoes don't go with my new dress, they're the wrong colour.*

gorgeous /'gɔ:dʒəs/ *adj* very nice or beautiful: *a gorgeous dress.*

gospel music /'gɒspəl mu:zɪk/ *n* a type of Christian music usually performed by black singers.

gross /grəʊs/ *adj* **1** very rude and offensive. **2** very bad and unacceptable.

guesthouse /'gesthaʊs/ *n* a private house where visitors may stay and have meals for payment.

guide /gaɪd/ *n* **1** a person who shows you round a place of interest or helps you to travel in a dangerous area: *They had a guide to show them the city | a mountain guide.* **2** a book that teaches you about something: *a guide for parents.*

Hh

hacker /'hækə/ *n* a person who spends a lot of time using a computer, especially one who secretly tries to use or change the information in someone else's computer.

hairstyle /'heəstaɪl/ *n* the style in which your hair is cut or arranged: *I like your new hairstyle.*

hamster /'hæmstə/ *n* a small animal with soft fur and no tail which is often kept as a pet.

handsome /'hænsəm/ *adj* nice to look at (usually used of men).

hard /hɑ:d/ *adv* a lot; very much: *It's raining hard. Are you working hard?*

headache /'hedeɪk/ *n* a pain in your head: *I've got a headache.*

headline /'hedlaɪn/ *n* words printed in large letters at the top of a newspaper story.

health /helθ/ *n* (no pl) how well your body is: *His health is not good (= he is often ill).*

healthy /'helθi/ *adj* **1** strong and well in your body: *healthy children | a healthy plant.* **2** good for your body: *It is healthy to eat fruit.*

heavy metal /ˌhevi 'metəl/ *n* a type of very loud rock music.

highly /'haɪli/ *adv* to a high or great degree: *highly paid; highly enjoyable.*

historical /hɪ'stɒrɪkəl/ *adj* in or about the past: *We cannot be sure whether King Arthur was a historical figure.*

hit /hɪt/ *n* **1** an act of touching something suddenly and forcefully: *I got a direct hit with my first shot.* **2** a song or film that is popular and successful: *That song was a hit last year.*

horrible /'hɒrəbəl/ *adj* very unpleasant or unkind

horror /'hɒrə/ *n* (no pl) great fear and shock: *I watched in horror as the cars crashed into each other. I like horror films.*

hospitable /'hɒspɪtəbəl/ *adj* being welcoming and kind to visitors.

house music /'haʊs 'mu:zɪk/ *n* a type of popular dance music.

however /haʊ'evə/ *adv* used when you are adding a piece of information which seems to disagree with what you have just said: *Normally he is a good student. However, his behaviour this week has been terrible.*

hurt /hɜ:t/ (**hurt, hurt, hurting**) *v* **1** to make yourself or someone else feel pain. **2** if part of your body hurts you feel pain in it: *My feet hurt after walking a long way yesterday.*

hypertext /'haɪpətekst/ *n* a word, phrase or icon which provides a link to another page or document on the Internet.

Ii

illegal /ɪ'li:gəl/ *adj* not allowed by law: *It is illegal to steal things.*

image /'ɪmɪdʒ/ *n* **1** a picture in the mind, or in a mirror: *He saw the image* of his face in the mirror. **2** the opinion which others have of one: *He will have to improve his image if he wants to be chosen.*

incredibly /ɪnˈkredɪbli/ *adv* very; extremely.

infect /ɪnˈfekt/ *v* to give an illness to someone: *One of the women at work had a cold and infected everyone else.*

influence /ˈɪnfluəns/ *n* an effect that someone or something has on events, behaviour or opinions: *He used his influence to get his son a job.*

influence /ˈɪnfluəns/ *v* to change what happens: *My teacher influenced my decision to study science.* (= made me decide to do it)

informal /ɪnˈfɔːməl/ *adj* happening or done in an easy, friendly way and not according to rules: *an informal meeting; an informal party.*

input /ˈɪnpʌt/ *n* information that is put into a computer.

instrument /ˈɪnstrəmənt/ *n* **1** a tool used for dong something special: *A pen is an instrument for writing.* **2** an object which is played to give musical sounds: *A piano is a musical instrument.*

instrumental /ˌɪnstrəˈmentl/ *adj* (of music) for instruments, not voices.

insurance /ɪnˈʃuərəns/ *n* (no pl) money paid to a company which then agrees to pay an amount of money if something bad happens to you or your property.

interested /ˈɪntrestɪd/ *adj* wanting to do something or know more about something: *He's very interested in history.*

the Internet /ði: ˈɪntənet/ *n* a system that allows people using computers around the world to exchange information.

invent /ɪnˈvent/ *v* to think of and plan something completely new that did not exist before: *Who invented the telephone?*

invention /ɪnˈvenʃən/ *n* something made, thought of or produced for the first time: *the invention of the telephone.*

island /ˈaɪlənd/ *n* a piece of land surrounded by water.

ivory /ˈaɪvəri/ *n* (no pl) hard, yellowish-white substance taken from tusks (= long teeth) of elephants.

Jj

jacket /ˈdʒækɪt/ *n* a short coat.

jeans /dʒiːnz/ *pl n* trousers made of strong cotton cloth, usually blue: *a pair of jeans.*

jersey /ˈdʒɜːzi/ *n* a piece of clothing, usually made of wool, that covers the top part of your body; a sweater.

jewellery /ˈdʒuːəlri/ *n* (no pl) jewels, gold, etc. made into rings, earrings and other ornaments.

junk food /ˈdʒʌŋk fuːd/ *n* bad quality food that is not good for you, especially because it contains a lot of chemicals.

Kk

keen /kiːn/ *adj* eager to do something; liking to do something: *He was keen to see the new film. Are you keen on swimming?*

keep up /ˌkiːp ʌp/ **(kept, kept, keeping)** *v* to remain level with: *I can't keep up with you when you walk so fast.*

keyboard /ˈkiːbɔːd/ *n* a row of keys on a musical instrument or a machine: *the keyboard of a piano/computer.*

kidnap /ˈkɪdnæp/ *v* to take someone away and ask for money for bringing them back safely.

kitchen /ˈkɪtʃən/ *n* a room used for preparing and cooking food.

Ll

lake /leɪk/ *n* a big pool of water with land all round it.

laser printer /ˈleɪzə ˌprɪntə/ *n* a machine, especially one connected to a computer system, that produces printed material by means of laser light.

laugh at /ˈlɑːf æt, ət/ *v* to treat a person or thing as very foolish, or make jokes about them: *They'll laugh at you if you wear that awful coat.*

leather /ˈleðə/ *n* (no pl) the skin of a dead animal specially prepared for use: *leather shoes.*

leech /liːtʃ/ *n* a small wormlike creature that lives by drinking the blood of living animals.

legal /ˈliːgəl/ *adj* allowed by the law: *Stealing is not legal.*

legality /lɪˈgæləti/ *n* the condition of being allowed by law.

library /ˈlaɪbrəri, -bri/ *n* a collection of books that people can borrow, or a room or building in which they are kept: *There's a very good library in the next town.*

lifestyle /ˈlaɪfstaɪl/ *n* the way in which you live, including the conditions you live in, the things you own and the things you do: *a healthy lifestyle; a fashionable lifestyle.*

light bulb /ˈlaɪt bʌlb/ *n* the glass part of an electric lamp that gives out light.

lighting engineer /ˈlaɪtɪŋ endʒɪˌnɪə/ *n* a person who is trained to control the lights for concerts, theatres or films.

lighting technician /ˈlaɪtɪŋ tekˌnɪʃən/ *n* a person who works with the lights for concerts, theatres or films.

liquid /ˈlɪkwɪd/ *n* a substance such as water which flows and is not solid or a gas.

look after /lʊk ɑːftə/ *v* to take care of someone or something: *She looked after my dog while I was on holiday.*

look for /ˈlʊk fɔː, fə/ *v* to try to find someone or something: *I'm looking for my key.*

look through /ˈlʊk θruː/ *v* to examine, especially for points to be noted.

luxury /ˈlʌkʃəri/ *n* **1** (no pl) great comfort: *They live in luxury in a very big house.* **2** something that you do not really need, but that is very pleasant: *Going to school in a car is a luxury.*

Mm

magical /ˈmædʒɪkəl/ *adj* strange and exciting: *It was a magical evening.*

magnet /ˈmægnɪt/ *n* a piece of iron that draws other pieces of iron towards it: *The magnet picked up the pins.*

magnetism /ˈmægnɪtɪzəm/ *n* (no pl) **1** the qualities of a magnet. **2** strong personal charm.

make-up /ˈmeɪk ʌp/ *n* (no pl) special coloured powder and creams that women sometimes put on their faces to make themselves look pretty.

manage /ˈmænɪdʒ/ *v* **1** to succeed in doing something: *He managed to avoid an accident.* **2** to control or be in charge of a business or activity: *He managed the supermarket when the owner was away.*

mansion /ˈmænʃən/ *n* a large house.

marijuana /ˌmærəˈwɑːnə/ *n* an illegal drug which is smoked.

mark /mɑːk/ *v* to say whether a piece of work is right or wrong or to show how good it is: *The teacher marked our examination papers.*

medicine /ˈmedsən/ *n* **1** (no pl) the study of treating and understanding illnesses: *A person who wants to become a doctor has to study medicine.* **2** something that you drink or eat when you are ill, to help you to get better.

medium /ˈmiːdiəm/ *adj* not big or small; of middle size or amount: *She is of medium height.*

microphone /ˈmaɪkrəfəʊn/ *n* an instrument for making sounds louder or recording them.

microscope /ˈmaɪkrəskəʊp/ *n* an instrument that helps you to see very small things by making them much bigger: *She looked at the insect under the microscope.*

microwave oven /ˈmaɪkrəweɪv ˌʌvən/ *n* a machine that cooks food very quickly by short wave radiation rather than by heat.

middle-aged /ˌmɪdl ˈeɪdʒd/ *adj* (used about people) between about forty and sixty years old.

mind /maɪnd/ *v* **1** to feel annoyed or upset about something. **2** not mind doing something to be willing to do something: *I don't mind driving if you're tired.*

miss /mɪs/ *v* **1** to feel sad because you cannot be with someone or something that you like: *I missed my dog when I lived in Spain.* **2** to be too late for something.

mixture /ˈmɪkstʃə/ *n* a number of different things or people put together: *This tea is a mixture of two different types.*

mobile phone /ˌməʊbaɪl ˈfəʊn/ *n* a telephone that you can carry with you wherever you go.

model /ˈmɒdl/ *v* (**modelled, modelled, modelling**) **1** to make a shape of something with a soft substance such as clay. **2** to wear new clothes at special shows so that people will see them and want to wear them.

modem /ˈməʊdəm, -dem/ *n* electronic equipment for sending information on computer via the telephone, radio, etc. to another distant computer.

monument /ˈmɒnjʊmənt/ *n* something that is built to help people to remember an important person or event.

mountain /ˈmaʊntən/ *n* a very high hill: *Mount Everest is the highest mountain in the world.*

mouse /maʊs/ *n* **1** (pl mice /maɪs/) a small animal with a long tail which lives in houses or in fields. **2** (pl **mouses** /ˈmaʊsɪz/) a small box, connected to a computer by a wire, which you move around on a surface in order to work the computer.

mug /mʌg/ *v* to rob with violence, especially in a dark street.

mugger /ˈmʌgə/ *n* a person who robs people with violence, especially in the street.

mugging /ˈmʌgɪŋ/ *n* robbing with violence, especially in a dark street.

murder /ˈmɜːdə/ *v* to kill a person on purpose when it is against the law.

murder /ˈmɜːdə/ *n* an act of killing another person when you have decided to do it: *Murder is a serious crime.*

murderer /ˈmɜːdərə/ *n* a person who kills someone on purpose when it is against the law.

muscle /ˈmʌsəl/ *n* one of the pieces of stretchy material in the body which can tighten to move parts of the body: *We use our muscles to move our arms and legs.*

museum /mjuːˈziːəm/ *n* a building in which you can see old, interesting or beautiful things: *the Museum of Modern Art.*

musician /mjuːˈzɪʃən/ *n* a person who plays an instrument or writes music.

Nn

neat /niːt/ *adj* **1** clean and well-arranged: *She always kept her room neat and tidy.* **2** careful and tidy: *her neat handwriting.*

notion /ˈnəʊʃən/ *n* an idea or belief.

nuclear fission /ˌnjuːkliə ˈfɪʃən/ *n* the very great power made by splitting the atom.

nylon /ˈnaɪlɒn/ *n* (no pl) a strong material, made by machines: *Nylon is used to make stockings and clothes.*

Oo

occasionally /əˈkeɪʒənəli/ *adv* happening from time to time.

offence /əˈfens/ *n* something that is wrong; a crime: *It is an offence to ride a bicycle at night without lights.*

often /ˈɒfən, ˈɒftən/ *adv* many times: *I often go to bed early.*

oil /ɔɪl/ *n* (no pl) thick liquid that comes from under the ground or under the sea, used for cooking, burning or for making machines work smoothly.

old-fashioned /ˌəʊld ˈfæʃənd/ *adj* not common any more: *old-fashioned clothes; old-fashioned ideas.*

operation /ˌɒpəˈreɪʃən/ *n* the cutting open of a part of the body of someone who is ill to make them better: *She needs an operation on her stomach.*

organic /ɔːˈgænɪk/ *adj* produced by or only found in animals or plants.

outfit /ˈaʊtfɪt/ *n* a set of clothes, especially for a special purpose: *I want to buy a new outfit because I'm going to a wedding.*

output /ˈaʊtpʊt/ *n* information or work produced by someone or something.

overcoat /ˈəʊvəkəʊt/ *n* a warm coat that you wear outside when it is cold.

overweight /ˌəʊvəˈweɪt/ *adj* too fat: *The doctor told her that she was overweight and should do more exercise.*

Pp

pain /peɪn/ *n* the feeling you have when part of your body hurts

painful /ˈpeɪnfəl/ *adj* hurt a lot: *His head was very painful.*

paragliding /ˈpærəglaɪdɪŋ/ *n* the sport of jumping from a height, attached to a kind of parachute which allows you to glide down to the ground.

paralysed /ˈpærəlaɪzd/ *adj* prevented from being able to move some or all of the body: *The climber was paralysed in a fall and couldn't walk.*

patient /ˈpeɪʃənt/ *n* a sick person who is being treated by a doctor: *There are 150 patients in the hospital.*

performance /pəˈfɔːməns/ *n* the acting of a part in a play or film in front of the public: *Her performance was very good.*

photocopier /ˈfəʊtəʊkɒpiə/ *n* a machine that makes photographic copies of a letter or a piece of writing.

physical /ˈfɪzɪkəl/ *adj* **1** concerning the body rather than the mind: *physical exercises.* **2** concerning things that you can see and touch.

physicist /ˈfɪzɪsɪst/ *n* a person who studies physics.

physics /ˈfɪzɪks/ *pl n* (used with a singular verb) the study of natural forces, such as heat, light and movement.

pill /pɪl/ *n* a small solid piece of medicine that you swallow.

plot /plɒt/ *n* **1** a secret plan by a group of people to do something wrong. **2** the story of a book, film, etc: *The film had an exciting plot.*

pocket calculator /ˌpɒkɪt ˈkælkjʊleɪtə/ *n* a small machine that can work out amounts using numbers.

pond /pɒnd/ *n* an area of water, smaller than a lake: *There's a duck pond in the middle of the village.*

poor /pɔː/ *adj* **1** not having much money: *She was too poor to buy clothes for the children.* **2** needing kindness or help: *The poor animal hasn't been fed.*

popular /ˈpɒpjʊlə/ *adj* liked by many people: *She is popular at school.*

popularity /ˌpɒpjʊˈlærəti/ *n* the quality or state of being liked by a lot of people.

poverty /ˈpɒvəti/ *n* the state of being poor: *She has lived in poverty all her life.*

prescribe /prɪˈskraɪb/ *v* to say what medicine or treatment a sick person must or should have: *The doctor prescribed a medicine for the child's stomach pains.*

pretty /ˈprɪti/ *adj* attractive and nice to look at: *a pretty girl | a pretty little village.*

printer /'prɪntə/ *n* a machine that prints computer information.

print out /'prɪnt aʊt/ *v* to produce a printed copy of a computer document.

process /'prəʊses/ *n* **1** a set of actions that you do in order to get a particular result: *Building a boat is not a simple process.* **2** a set of changes that happen naturally: *a chemical process.*

produce /prə'dju:s/ *v* **1** to make something, especially in large quantities: *The factory produces 500 cars a week.* **2** to control the organisation of a play or film for the public to see.

producer /prə'dju:sə/ *n* a person who produces a play or film.

product /'prɒdʌkt/ *n* something that is produced in a factory: *plastic products.*

pull over /ˌpʊl 'əʊvə/ *v* (of a vehicle) to move over to one side of the road.

punish /'pʌnɪʃ/ *v* to make someone suffer because they have done something wrong: *The teacher punished the noisy children by making them stay after school.*

put on /ˌpʊt 'ɒn/ *v* to cover the body with, especially clothes; get dressed in: *He put his coat on.*

puzzle /'pʌzəl/ *n* **1** a person or thing which you cannot understand or explain: *It's a puzzle where all my money goes every week.* **2** a game or toy which is difficult to do: *Can you do this jigsaw puzzle?*

Rr

rafting /'ra:ftɪŋ/ *n* a sport in which you travel across water on a wooden or rubber floating structure like a boat.

rap /ræp/ *n* a style of popular black music with a strong beat and with words recited, not sung.

rarely /'reəli/ *adv* not very often: *She is old and rarely goes out.*

reach /ri:tʃ/ *v* to get to a place or arrive at a place: *They reached London on Thursday. She's reached the age when she can leave school.*

really /'rɪəli/ *adv* in fact or very much: *I am really worried about my work. He is really nice.*

reggae /'regeɪ/ *n* a type of popular music from the West Indies with a strong regular beat.

release /rɪ'li:s/ *v* to let someone or something go: *I released the horse and it ran away. Four prisoners were released.*

relax /rɪ'læks/ *v* to become less worried, angry, tight, etc.: *Don't worry about it; just try to relax.*

research /rɪ'sɜ:tʃ/ *n* (no pl) careful study, especially to find out something new: *scientific research; medical research.*

research /rɪ'sɜ:tʃ/ *v* to study something to find out new things.

reservation /ˌrezə'veɪʃən/ *n* an arrangement to make sure that something is kept for your use: *Have you made a reservation at the hotel?*

reserve /rɪ'zɜ:v/ *v* to keep something for someone or arrange for something to be kept: *I have reserved a table for us at the restaurant.*

rhythm and blues /ˌrɪðəm ən 'blu:z/ *n* a type of black American popular music which started in the 1940s.

ring /rɪŋ/ *n* a round band, especially of gold or silver, worn on the finger.

rob /rɒb/ *v* (**robbed, robbed, robbing**) to take something from a person, bank or shop when it is not yours: *They planned to rob a bank.*

robber /'rɒbə/ *n* a person who steals something from a person, a bank or a shop: *a bank robber.*

robbery /'rɒbəri/ *n* the crime of stealing something from a person, a bank or a shop: *a bank robbery.*

rock 'n' roll /ˌrɒk ən 'rəʊl/ *n* popular modern dance music, played on electric instruments.

rocky /'rɒki/ *adj* covered with rocks, large pieces of stone: *a rocky path.*

romantic /rəʊ'mæntɪk, rə-/ *n* showing feelings of love.

rope /rəʊp/ *n* a strong thick cord.

rough /rʌf/ *adj* **1** not smooth; uneven: *a rough surface.* **2** not calm or gentle: *The sea was rough in the storm.* **3** not finished: *a rough drawing.*

ruin /'ru:ɪn/ *n* **1** a building that has been almost destroyed: *There was a ruin on the top of the hill.* **2 ruins** *pl n* the remaining parts of a destroyed building: *We saw the ruins of the church.*

Ss

sad /sæd/ *adj* unhappy: *She felt very sad that the holiday was ending.*

sadness /'sædnɪs/ *n* a feeling of unhappiness.

sailing /'seɪlɪŋ/ *n* the sport of travelling in or directing a small boat with sails.

sand /sænd/ *n* **1** (no pl) fine powder, usually white or yellow, made of rock, often found next to the sea and in deserts. **sands** *pl n* places covered with sand.

sandy /'sændi/ *adj* covered with sand: *a sandy shore.*

satellite /'sætəlaɪt/ *n* **1** something which moves round the Earth or another planet: *The moon is a satellite of the Earth.* **2** an object sent into space to receive signals from one part of the world and send them to another: *The television broadcast came from America by satellite.*

savings /'seɪvɪŋz/ *pl n* money that you keep without spending: *He used his savings to buy a bicycle.*

saxophone /'sæksəfəʊn/ *n* a metal musical instrument which is played by blowing into it and pressing keys, used especially in jazz music.

scan /skæn/ *v* **1** to look quickly at something written, without reading it carefully, often looking for a particular thing: *He scanned the list of names, looking for someone he knew.* **2** to examine something closely, especially because you are looking for something: *The soldiers were scanning the sky for planes.*

science /'saɪəns/ *n* the study of nature and the way things in the world are made and behave.

science fiction /ˌsaɪəns 'fɪkʃən/ *n* stories about imaginary worlds or imaginary scientific developments.

scientific /ˌsaɪən'tɪfɪk/ *adj* of or about science: *scientific studies.*

scientist /'saɪəntɪst/ *n* a person who studies or practises science.

scratch /skrætʃ/ *n* **1** to make marks with something sharp: *The stick scratched the side of the car.* **2** to rub your nails lightly over a part of your body: *Don't scratch those mosquito bites; they'll feel worse.*

screen /skri:n/ *n* a flat, square surface on which information or pictures can be shown: *a television screen | a computer screen.*

script /skrɪpt/ *n* a written form of a speech, play, film or broadcast: *Have the actors got their scripts yet?*

scriptwriter /'skrɪptˌraɪtə/ *n* a person who writes the script for a film or broadcast.

scuba diving /'sku:bə ˌdaɪvɪŋ/ *n* a sport in which you swim underwater with a container of air on your back, breathing through a tube.

seafood /'si:fu:d/ *n* sea creatures that you eat.

secure /sɪ'kjʊə/ *adj* **1** safe; not likely to be stolen or taken away. **2** fixed firmly; that will not move or fall easily.

Mini-dictionary

secretary /'sekrətəri/ *n* a person who does office work, writes letters, etc. for an employer.

sentence /'sentəns/ *n* 1 a group of words which makes a statement or a question. 2 a punishment for a criminal.

sequel /'si:kwəl/ *n* 1 a book or film which continues the action of an earlier one. 2 something that follows something else, especially as a result.

set /set/ *n* a place where a film or TV programme is filmed.

set manager /'set ,mænɪdʒə/ *n* a person who organises the scenery for a play or film.

shirt /ʃɜːt/ *n* a piece of clothing with buttons down the front that covers the upper part of the body and your arms.

shock /ʃɒk/ *v* to cause unpleasant or angry surprise.

shoe /ʃuː/ *n* something you wear on your foot when you go outside: *a pair of shoes.*

shoot /ʃuːt/ *v* (shot, shot, shooting) 1 to fire at something or someone with a gun. 2 to make a film: *This film was shot in London.*

shoplift /'ʃɒp,lɪft/ *v* to take things from a shop without paying for them.

shoplifter /'ʃɒp,lɪftə/ *n* a person who takes things from a shop without paying for them.

shoplifting /'ʃɒp,lɪftɪŋ/ *n* taking things from a shop without paying for them: *She was caught shoplifting.*

sick /sɪk/ *adj* 1 suffering from a disease or illness. 2 to vomit.

signal /'sɪgnəl/ *n* a movement or thing that tells you what to do: *The railway signal showed that the train could pass.*

silicon chip /'sɪlɪkən tʃɪp/ *n* a small electronic part used in a computer.

sinister /'sɪnɪstə/ *adj* threatening evil.

size /saɪz/ *n* how big someone or something is: *What size is your house? The two books were the same size. These shoes are size 5.*

skiing /'skiːɪŋ/ *n* the sport of travelling on snow with skis, long narrow pieces of wood, plastic or metal, on your feet.

skin /skɪn/ *n* the outside of a person, animal, vegetable or fruit: *You can make shoes from the skins of animals | a banana skin. She has pale skin.*

skin /skɪn/ *v* to remove the skin from something.

skirt /skɜːt/ *n* a piece of woman's clothing that hangs from her waist and covers part of her legs.

sky /skaɪ/ *n* the space above the Earth which you can see if you look up.

slave /sleɪv/ *n* a person who is owned by another person and has to work for him and has no freedom: *A long time ago, black people were taken to America as slaves.*

sleeping bag /'sliːpɪŋ bæg/ *n* a large bag which you sleep in to keep warm, usually when you are sleeping outdoors.

slim /slɪm/ *adj* thin in an attractive way: *He's tall and slim.*

slip /slɪp/ *v* (slipped, slipped, slipping) 1 to slide on a smooth surface by accident: *He slipped on the ice and fell.* 2 to move quickly, smoothly or quietly: *She slipped out of the room when nobody was looking.*

smart /smɑːt/ *adj* dressed in good, clean clothes: *My sister always looks smart. She always wears smart clothes.*

smuggle /'smʌgəl/ *v* to bring things into a country secretly without paying the money that should be paid: *He was caught smuggling cameras into the country. n* **smuggling**

smuggler /'smʌglə/ *n* a person who breaks the law by bringing things secretly into a country: *drugs smugglers.*

sock /sɒk/ *n* a soft piece of clothing you wear on your foot and the bottom part of your leg.

solo /'səʊləʊ/ *n* a piece of music played or sung by one person.

sometimes /'sʌmtaɪmz/ *adv* at times; now and then: *We sometimes go to the cinema, but not very often.*

sophisticated /sə'fɪstɪkeɪtɪd/ *adj* experienced in social life and behaviour: *a sophisticated young woman.*

sore /sɔː/ *adj* painful: *a sore throat.*

sort out /,sɔːt 'aʊt/ *v* to put things in order; to solve.

soul music /'səʊl ,mjuːzɪk/ *n* a type of popular music which often expresses deep emotions.

sound technician /'saʊnd tek,nɪʃən/ *n* a skilled person who works on the sound effects of a film.

special effects /,speʃəl ɪ'fekts/ *pl n* in film and television, special lighting, sound, camerawork and computer graphics.

spectacular /spek'tækjʊlə/ *adj* very special; causing admiration: *a spectacular view from the top of the mountain.*

spectacularly /spek'tækjʊləli/ *adv* in a very special way, causing admiration: *The film was spectacularly successful.*

spiky /'spaɪki/ *adj* having long points: *He's got spiky hair.*

sprain /spreɪn/ *v* to damage a joint of your body by turning it suddenly: *He sprained his ankle when he fell.*

spring /sprɪŋ/ *n* 1 the season after winter, in cool countries, when plants start to grow again. 2 a river coming up from the ground. 3 a twisted round piece of metal wire which you can find inside a bed, etc.

spy /spaɪ/ *n* a person whose job is to discover secret information, usually about another country.

stand /stænd/ *v* (stood, stood, standing) 1 to be on your feet in an upright position 2 can't stand to hate someone or something: *I can't stand dogs.*

steal /stiːl/ *v* (stole, stolen, stealing) to take something that does not belong to you, without asking for it: *Who stole my money?*

stick /stɪk/ *n* 1 a long thin piece of wood. 2 a thin piece of wood which some people use to help them to walk: *Granny has to walk with a stick now.*

stick up /,stɪk 'ʌp/ *v* (stuck, stuck, sticking) to come out straight upwards: *His hair always sticks up in the morning.*

stony /'stəʊni/ *adj* covered with stones, small pieces of rock.

stress /stres/ *n* 1 (no pl) a state of difficulty: *The stress of working for examinations made him ill.* 2 (pl **stresses**) saying a word or a part of a word with special force: *In the word 'chemistry' the stress is on the first part of the word.*

strict /strɪkt/ *adj* severe and very firm, especially about behaviour: *They are very strict with their children.*

string /strɪŋ/ *n* 1 (no pl) thin rope used for fastening things: *The parcel was tied with string.* 2 a fine piece of wire used in some musical instruments, such as a violin.

style /staɪl/ *n* 1 a way of doing something: *a hair style.* 2 the way of dressing that everyone likes at a special time: *That dress is in the latest style.* 3 a sort or type: *a new style of car.*

success /sək'ses/ *n* 1 (no pl) the act of doing or getting what you hoped for: *his success in the examination.* 2 (pl **successes**) someone or something that pleases people or does well: *Her party was a great success.*

successful /sək'sesfəl/ *adj* having done something one has tried to do: *Making my cake was very successful.*

suffer /'sʌfə/ *v* to be in pain or trouble: *She was suffering from a headache.*

suit /suːt, sjuːt/ *n* a set of clothes made from the same material, including a short coat with trousers or skirt: *a dark suit.*

suit /suːt, sjuːt/ *v* **1** to be right or convenient for someone: *It's a small house but it suits our needs.* **2** to make someone look good: *That dress suits you.*

sunbathe /'sʌnbeɪð/ *v* to lie in the sun to make your body brown. *n* **sunbathing**

sunglasses /'sʌnˌglɑːsɪz/ *pl n* glasses with dark glass in them which you wear when it is very sunny and bright.

sunny /'sʌni/ *adj* full of bright sunlight: *The day was bright and sunny.*

suntan /'sʌntæn/ *n* the brownness of the skin after the effects of sunshine.

superstar /'suːpəstɑː, sjuː-/ *n* an extremely famous performer, especially a singer or a film actor.

surgery /'sɜːdʒəri/ *n* **1** (no pl) the cutting open of a part of a person's body to mend parts inside them. **2** a place where you can go to see a doctor.

swimming pool /'swɪmɪŋ puːl/ *n* a place where people can go to swim.

symptom /'sɪmptəm/ *n* a sign of something, especially an illness: *Fever is a symptom of many illnesses.*

Tt

tacky /'tæki/ *adj* unpleasant and of poor quality.

take out /ˌteɪk 'aʊt/ *v* (**took, taken, taking**) to remove something: *The dentist took out the bad tooth.*

taste /teɪst/ *n* **1** the special sense by which we know one food from another: *My sense of taste is not very good; I have a cold.* **2** the feeling that a particular food gives you when it is in your mouth: *Chocolate has a sweet taste.* **3** someone's particular choice: *She has good taste in clothes.*

tattoo /tə'tuː, tæ'tuː/ *v* to make a pattern on the skin by pricking it and putting colouring substances on it.

technician /tek'nɪʃən/ *n* a person who works with machines or instruments: *Anne is training to be a technician.*

technique /tek'niːk/ *n* a way of doing something new: *new teaching techniques.*

techno pop /'teknəʊ pɒp/ *n* a type of popular, electronic dance music.

technology /tek'nɒlədʒi/ *n* (no pl) knowledge about science, and about the making of certain machines or instruments: *Modern technology has made many jobs easier.*

teddy boy /'tedi bɔɪ/ *n* in Britain, especially in the 1950s, a young man who dressed in a style similar to that of the early 20th century, wearing a long loose jacket, narrow trousers and thick soft shoes.

telescope /'telɪskəʊp/ *n* an instrument that you look through to see objects that are very small or far away from you.

temperature /'temprətʃə/ *n* the amount of heat or cold: *In hot weather the temperature gets very high. When I was ill, I had a high temperature; I felt very hot.*

test /test/ *v* **1** to look at something to see if it is correct or will work properly: *Before he bought the car, he drove it to test it.* **2** to ask someone questions to see if they know the answers: *The teacher tested the children on their homework.*

test /test/ *n* an examination: *I passed my driving test | a history test | an eye test | a blood test.*

thief /θiːf/ *n* (pl **thieves**) someone who steals things.

thin /θɪn/ *adj* **1** narrow; not thick: *This string is too thin.* **2** not having much fat on your body: *You should eat more; you're too thin.*

think of /'θɪŋk əv/ *v* (**thought, thought, thinking**) to consider the idea of doing something.

thriller /'θrɪlə/ *n* a book, play or film that tells a very exciting story, usually of crime and violence.

throat /θrəʊt/ *n* **1** the part at the back of your mouth, where you swallow: *He couldn't speak because he had a sore throat.* **2** the front part of your neck.

tidiness /'taɪdɪnɪs/ *n* neatness.

tidy /'taɪdi/ *adj* in good order, with things neatly arranged: *a tidy room.*

tie /taɪ/ *n* a narrow band of cloth worn around the neck, especially by a man.

tight /taɪt/ *adj* **1** pulled or drawn closely together: *a very tight knot.* **2** fitting part of your body closely: *These shoes are too tight.*

tights /taɪts/ *pl n* a very tight piece of clothing, made of thin material, which women wear to cover their feet, legs and the lower part of their body: *a pair of tights.*

tongue-tied /'tʌŋ taɪd/ *adj* unable to speak freely because you are nervous.

tool /tuːl/ *n* an instrument which helps us to do work.

tour /tʊə/ *n* **1** a journey during which several places are visited: *They have gone on a tour.* **2** a trip to or through a place: *We went on a tour of the city.*

tour /tʊə/ *v* to visit many different parts of a country or an area.

tourist /'tʊərɪst/ *n* a person who travels for pleasure.

tradition /trə'dɪʃən/ *n* an old custom passed on from parents to their children: *an old family tradition.*

traditional /trə'dɪʃənəl/ *adj* done in the same way for a long time: *a traditional family Christmas.*

train /treɪn/ *v* to make yourself, or someone else, ready to do something difficult: *I am training for the race. She is training to become a nurse. He trains horses.*

trainers /'treɪnəz/ *n* strong shoes with a heavy rubber bottom used for sport.

transport /'trænspɔːt/ *n* (no pl) **1** the moving of goods or people from one place to another. **2** cars, buses, trains, etc.

treat /triːt/ *v* **1** to behave towards: *He treated the animal cruelly.* **2** to give medicine as a doctor: *to treat an illness.* **3** to give someone something special: *I'm going to treat myself to a new coat.*

treatment /'triːtmənt/ *n* the act, manner or method of treating someone: *He's gone to hospital for special treatment.*

trendy /'trendi/ *adj* very fashionable.

trumpet /'trʌmpɪt/ *n* a musical instrument made of brass that you play by blowing through it.

try on /ˌtraɪ 'ɒn/ *v* to put on a piece of clothing to see if it fits you.

T-shirt /'tiː ʃɜːt/ *n* a piece of clothing with a round neck and short sleeves which you usually wear in summer.

Uu

unattractive /ˌʌnə'træktɪv/ *adj* not causing pleasure; not beautiful; not attractive: *an unattractive industrial area of the city.*

unconventional /ˌʌnkən'venʃənəl/ *adj* unusual; not following the custom: *unconventional clothes.*

unconvincing /ˌʌnkən'vɪnsɪŋ/ *adj* not easy to believe or accept: *an unconvincing excuse.*

unfashionable /ˌʌn'fæʃənəbəl/ *adj* a way of dressing that does not follow the style popular at that particular time.

uninspiring /ˌʌnɪn'spaɪərɪŋ/ *adj* does not encourage you to do something; not inspiring.

unique /juː'niːk/ *adj* the only one of its type: *a unique chance to see inside the palace.*

Mini-dictionary

unsuccessful /ˌʌnsəkˈsesfəl/ *adj* not having the result you aimed for: *an unsuccessful attempt to rescue a cat.*

untidiness /ʌnˈtaɪdɪnes/ *adj* the state of being untidy or not neat.

untidy /ʌnˈtaɪdi/ *adj* in disorder; not neat: *Her room was ever so untidy - there were clothes all over the floor.*

upbringing /ˈʌpbrɪŋɪŋ/ *n* the way someone is cared for and taught to behave by their parents: *They had a very strict upbringing.*

Vv

VDU /ˌviː diː ˈjuː/ *n* (visual display unit) the part of a computer which shows information on a screen.

violin /ˌvaɪəˈlɪn/ *n* a musical instrument with four strings, played with a bow.

virtual reality /ˌvɜːtʃuəl riˈæləti/ *n* a computer image with which a user can interact in a realistic way.

Ww

war /wɔː/ *n* a time of fighting between countries: *a prisoner of war.*

weak /wiːk/ *adj* **1** not strong in body or character: *She was weak after her illness.* **2** containing a lot of water: *This tea is very weak.*

wealthy /ˈwelθi/ *adj* rich; having a lot of money: *a wealthy family.*

well /wel/ *adv* (**better, best**) in a good or satisfactory way: *Mary can't read very well.*

well-built /ˌwel bɪlt/ *adj* having a strong body with large muscles.

western /ˈwestən/ *n* a story or film about life in the West of the United States in the past.

wildlife reserve /ˈwaɪldlaɪf rɪˌzɜːv/ *n* a place where wild animals can live safely.

windsurfing /ˈwɪndsɜːfɪŋ/ *n* the sport of moving along on the water on a flat board with a sail.

wind up /ˌwaɪnd ˈʌp/ *v* (**wound, wound, winding**) to turn part of a machine round and round in order to make it work: *He wound up his watch.*

window-shop /ˈwɪndəʊ ʃɒp/ *v* to look at the goods in shop windows without intending to buy anything.

winner /ˈwɪnə/ *n* a person who comes first or does best in a competition, race or fight.

wipe /waɪp/ *v* to make something dry or clean with a cloth: *Will you wipe the table?*

wolf /wʊlf/ *n* (pl **wolves**) a wild animal of the dog family which hunts other animals in a group.

wonderful /ˈwʌndəfəl/ *adj* very good: *wonderful news.*

wool /wʊl/ *n* **1** the soft thick hair of a sheep **2** the soft thick thread or cloth which is made from the hair of a sheep.

woollen /ˈwʊlən/ *adj* made of wool: *a woollen dress.*

worried /ˈwʌrid/ *adj* anxious: *He seems worried about something.*

worth /wɜːθ/ *prep* **1** with a value of: *This bicycle is worth £50.* **2** good enough or useful enough: *That film is worth seeing.*

WWW /ˈwɜːld ˈwaɪd ˈweb/ *n* (World Wide Web) a system which connects information and pictures from computers in many parts of the world so that people can find them on the Internet.

Xx

X-ray /ˈeks reɪ/ *n* a photograph of the inside of your body, taken with a special light which cannot normally be seen, and used by a doctor: *The X-ray showed that the boy's leg was broken.*

Yy

yacht /jɒt/ *n* **1** a boat with sails. **2** a big motor-boat that people can live and travel in on holiday or race in.

Irregular verb list

Infinitive	Past simple	Past participle
be	was/were	been
begin	began	begun
bend	bent	bent
bite	bit	bitten
break	broke	broken
bring	brought	brought
build	built	built
buy	bought	bought
catch	caught	caught
choose	chose	chosen
come	came	come
cost	cost	cost
cut	cut	cut
do	did	done
draw	drew	drawn
dream	dreamt/dreamed	dreamt/dreamed
drink	drank	drunk
drive	drove	driven
eat	ate	eaten
fall	fell	fallen
feed	fed	fed
feel	felt	felt
fight	fought	fought
find	found	found
fly	flew	flown
forget	forgot	forgotten
get	got	got
give	gave	given
go	went	gone
grow	grew	grown
have	had	had
hear	heard	heard
hide	hid	hidden
hit	hit	hit
hold	held	held
hurt	hurt	hurt
keep	kept	kept
know	knew	known
lay	laid	laid
learn	learnt/learned	learnt/learned
leave	left	left
lose	lost	lost
make	made	made
mean	meant	meant
meet	met	met
pay	paid	paid
put	put	put
read	read	read
ride	rode	ridden
ring	rang	rung
run	ran	run
say	said	said
see	saw	seen
sell	sold	sold
send	sent	sent

Infinitive	Past simple	Past participle
shine	shone	shone
shoot	shot	shot
show	showed	shown/showed
sing	sang	sung
sink	sank	sunk
sit	sat	sat
sleep	slept	slept
speak	spoke	spoken
spell	spelt	spelt
spend	spent	spent
stand	stood	stood
steal	stole	stolen
stick	stuck	stuck
swim	swam	swum
take	took	taken
teach	taught	taught
tell	told	told
think	thought	thought
throw	threw	thrown
understand	understood	understood
wake (up)	woke (up)	woken (up)
wear	wore	worn
win	won	won
write	wrote	written

Phonetic chart

CONSONANTS

SYMBOL	KEYWORD
/ p /	pen
/ b /	back
/ t /	tea
/ d /	day
/ k /	key
/ g /	got
/ tʃ /	cheer
/ dʒ /	jump
/ f /	fat
/ v /	video
/ θ /	thing
/ ð /	then
/ s /	soon
/ z /	zoo
/ ʃ /	fish
/ʒ /	pleasure
/ h /	hot
/ m /	come
/ n /	sun
/ ŋ /	sung
/ l /	led
/ r/	red
/ j /	yet
/ w /	wet

VOWEL

SYMBOL	KEYWORD
/ iː /	sheep
/ ɪ /	ship
/ e /	bed
/ æ /	bad
/ aː /	calm
/ o /	pot
/ ɔː /	saw
/ ʊ /	put
/ uː /	boot
/ ʌ /	cut
/ ɜː /	bird
/ ə /	ago

DIPHTHONGS

SYMBOL	KEYWORD
/ eɪ /	make
/ əʊ /	note
/ aɪ /	bite
/ aʊ /	now
/ ɔɪ /	boy
/ ɪə /	here
/ eə /	there
/ ʊə /	tour